60 Miles
MY TRIALS AND SMILES

SOPHIE JOHNSON

60 Miles
My Trials and Smiles

Copyright © Diana Forsyth 2016 All Rights Reserved

The rights of Diana Forsyth to be identified as the author of this work have been asserted in accordance with the Copyright, Designs and Patents Act 1988

All rights reserved. No part may be reproduced, adapted, stored in a retrieval system or transmitted by any means, electronic, mechanical, photocopying, or otherwise without the prior written permission of the author or publisher.

Spiderwize
Remus House
Coltsfoot Drive
Woodston
Peterborough
PE2 9BF

www.spiderwize.com

A CIP catalogue record for this book is available from the British Library.

The views expressed in this work are solely those of the author and do not necessarily reflect the views of the publisher, and the publisher hereby disclaims any responsibility for them.

I am dedicating this book to my very dear friend Kath who sadly lost her battle with cancer on July 9th 2015

INTRODUCTION

As a girl growing up I never had much ambition. I only ever wanted to be a housewife and mother, spending my days running the home and looking after my children.

I was a child of the 50s having been born in 1954 and although that ambition seems silly by today's standards I don't think it was that unusual for the day. Of course today's youngsters want it all. They want to have successful careers, travel the world and settle down and have their family much later. It was much more common in the 50s for the woman to stay at home and raise the children herself, rather than going out and forging a career. I guess as my mother did just that I was copying her, but it was genuinely all I ever wanted. I never even went to university like so many of the children do nowadays. In the early 1970s it was an option but by no means as common as today. In my day I guess most of the university places were taken up by children from the grammar schools. As for leaving university with huge debts, the idea would have been abhorrent to me, as the only acceptable loan was a mortgage! However, I'm sure many children from my school did later achieve the grades necessary for university when they went on to do their A levels at college. As for me, I left school at 16 and got a job for Barclays Bank, where I worked for 10 happy years.

One day, while working there, a tall, handsome, dark-haired young man came in and started to 'chat me up'. Well, I'm not sure he was chatting me up, it was more that he was talking a lot about himself, but there was something about him that made me laugh. He didn't have two heads or anything, it was just that he had a very sharp wit and was a really amusing guy. I found out his name was Peter, a name I found a little too starchy, so from then on he became known as Pete to me, although always Peter to his family. Pete was great, and we often met for lunch as he worked nearby as a Civil Engineer. We used to go to the local recreation ground and have sandwiches together, sitting on the grass and enjoying the sunshine throughout the summer. Such happy days! It was very important to me that my family liked Pete, and I'm pleased to say that they loved him. Due to his easy manner, sense of humour and kindness he was an easy man to love. As time passed we moved in together and eventually Pete proposed to me. My response was to burst into tears as I was just so happy! I believe I did manage to mutter 'yes' amongst my sobs!

A summer wedding followed in June 1979 which I remember as a simply lovely day when I've never felt happier. The sun shone and I just couldn't stop smiling. All of our family and friends were there to watch us take our vows. I was very nervous as I walked up the aisle with my dad, John, but bless him he was even more nervous than I was! My mum looked gorgeous in a lovely cream suit which she had bought knowing she would have to lose some weight to make sure she looked her best. She struggled for weeks to lose weight, but she succeeded! There's nothing like an incentive to spur you on to your goal! The day passed all too fast and after a two week honeymoon in Tenerife we settled down to normal, everyday married life.

With the birth of our first son Marcus, who was born in August 1981, our happiness felt complete. I filled my days doting over our new baby and making sure my husband had a nice hot meal to come home to after work. Harry was born the following year in December 1982. The next five years passed with the normal ups and downs of family life. I felt very happy with my life and blessed to have such a lovely family. When Harry started school I got a part-time job, but always had a niggling feeling in the back of my mind that I'd like to extend my family, as I had always wanted four children. Pete was very happy with the idea (being the youngest of four children himself) and in June 1989 we welcomed Felix into the world! As Marcus and Harry were so close in age they were great friends and played together all the time, so it seemed only fair that Felix should have a playmate as well! Freddie was born in February 1991. Now my family was truly complete, four boys – how lovely! Sometimes I think it would have been nice to have had a girl but with four boys I must admit I am spoiled rotten! Family life was certainly busy but interesting, as you watch each of your children develop into their own little person. When Felix was at playschool it was obvious he was far shorter than the other children. We took him to the doctors who referred him to hospital, where it was discovered that he had a growth hormone deficiency. We were told he would have to have daily injections for the foreseeable future.

This was a huge shock for the family, but we rallied round as families do, and did all we could to help him. Felix was only four years old, but the hospital told us that without the injections he may only grow to 4 foot 10 inches! We really had no choice but to inject him. In time Felix learnt to give himself the injections, and he was brilliant, but his growth was astonishing! Felix is now 25 and he is 6 foot tall which confirms that we did make the right decision!

When Felix was about to go into secondary school I took him and Freddie along to an opticians for an eye test. Freddie was fine, but Felix could not read any of the eye chart with his left eye, so again we were referred to the hospital. Many tests later it was discovered that Felix had a brain tumour which was wrapped around his optic nerve!

Can you imagine the shock? We had so many questions, but were left reeling as the doctors told us the tumour was inoperable because of its position. They did confirm though that the tumour was the cause of his growth hormone deficiency. For his sake we did our utmost to stay positive. It was a lot to take in, and we tried hard to hide our worries and concerns from Felix. The poor lad had to manage with only one eye, but there were lots of people in the world with only one eye and they seem to manage okay. As far as Felix was concerned, it was just as it had always been, but now because of the tumour we would be under the doctor's care for the foreseeable future. Thankfully, the doctors told us that they were as confident as they could be that the tumour wasn't growing. They said that Felix would have had sight in only one eye from birth and his other eye would be compensating for the loss. As a mother, I felt bad for not realising my son was only sighted in one eye until he was 11. How could I not have realised?

So family life continued with Pete and I always keeping a watchful eye over Felix. His brothers made no compensations at all, but that's how Felix wanted it. He was a strong lad and determined not to be singled out as being different. What proud parents we were!

I remember back to my school days having the chance to go on a day trip to France, and I was so excited I could hardly contain myself. My boys by comparison had several trips abroad to enhance their school studies and thought nothing of it. When they got to 6th form college Marcus had the opportunity to go to Mexico for a month and jumped at the chance. Harry had the chance to go to Africa (can't remember where now) but being a real home lover, who enjoyed his creature comforts, he chose not to go. A few years later Freddie travelled to Costa Rica for a month for his college trip and absolutely loved it. Felix, like Harry, opted out but he did go to Valencia for three months to learn some basic Spanish. Quite a hard thing to do on your own! He arrived in Spain, knew no-one at all, and couldn't speak the language! I feel this demonstrates what a strong lad he is, and we really admired him!

During these years I tried several part time jobs as it was important to me to do more than just 'keep house'. Pete had a degree and was progressing well in the company he worked for. As for me, I had always yearned to have some sort of proper qualification so for five years I went to evening school and studied for one GCSE per year. The plan was to then do two A-levels and maybe then an Open University course. I managed the one A-level but I don't know what happened, I never did get the second one! I guess life just got in the way! I have always felt that I am capable of doing more than I do and fortunately I am blessed with loads of energy and drive. The boys all went to university but Felix admits he didn't work as hard as he could have done and certainly didn't achieve his potential. What a shame! Both Marcus and Harry I'm sure would say the same if I asked them! I remember Harry going without sleep for days as the due date for his dissertation loomed! Honestly – boys!

Life is of course supposed to be a series of ups and downs but in 2011 and 2012 we had a really horrible time as a family. In February 2011 my dear Pete was charged with a corporate offence and given a prison sentence of 21 months! Prisoners only serve half of their sentences so in his case he had to serve six and a half months in custody and then he was released with a tag for the remaining time. Pete is not a dishonest man but as the Managing Director of a company the buck stopped with him, although he personally did nothing wrong at all! It seemed unfair, but that's how it was and he handled it well, accepting his fate with dignity.

I was kept busy with visiting and arranging visits for his friends and choir members as he was a popular member of our local Choral Society. Of course I was also writing letters to him, but it was hard for him to reply because he didn't really have any 'news' to tell me. Sometimes the letters were opened so after a while we stopped the letter writing and had frequent phone calls instead.

The boys outwardly coped with it very well but you don't really know what's going on inside their heads do you? Between us we all pulled together and kept things on an even keel. Pete and I enjoyed our visits even though the situation seemed surreal – I couldn't bear to leave him there when it was time to say goodbye. That was the hardest bit. I kept hanging by the door for a last wave and Pete kept hanging back, always being the last person to leave the visiting room just so we could grab a few more precious seconds. It was hard. The one and a half hour journey home was spent deep in thought, it's a wonder I ever got home safely at all! I think sometimes when we drive we are on automatic pilot. I remember getting home and having no memory of traffic lights I went through – did I look at all? Were they green? I always did get home safely, so my guardian angel must have been looking over me!

I had mixed emotions as Pete's release date in September 2011 drew near, but I knew we had a strong marriage and was hopeful all would be well. He was of course delighted to be free, but for a while we danced on eggshells around one another, both of us being over-anxious to please. It was a difficult time for all of us and it made me think how awful it must be for prisoners who have lengthy sentences – I would guess that some marriages just don't survive! Pete slowly gained confidence and started to feel more relaxed although clearly carrying a fair bit of anger over his situation as he felt it was so unjust!

Yet again life slipped back into some sort of normality. I felt quite strongly that it must otherwise we could never move on, and that way whatever was causing the stress has won. It really is important to 'let things go' and to remember that life is very short.

Life was not about to get easier though, as the New Year of 2012 made its presence felt by robbing us of Pete's dad in the January, followed by dear Felix suffering a brain haemorrhage in the March, and then my mum passing away in the July! As a family we were knocked sideways and just couldn't believe how much bad luck we had had! Unfortunately Felix lost a bit more of his eyesight and had his driving licence taken away. I feel so desperately sorry for him, but we remain positive and hope advances in medical science will one day find a way to let him drive again – that's my dream! I have often thought about fundraising to help Felix but it's not a question of money (if only it were that simple), it's finding a doctor who can help him... Maybe in the future who knows!

Life has certainly had its challenges for the whole family but particularly for Pete and Felix. With my 60th birthday looming I felt I wanted to do something challenging for myself, a positive challenge, that's what I needed. I was mulling it over while on holiday at the Dartmouth Music Festival with friends last year and thinking of 60 ways to do what? My friend Angie suddenly blurted out, 'How about 60 ways to travel a mile?' It was one of those 'eureka' moments – I absolutely loved the idea! Our friends Geoff, Angie and I started coming up with ideas. The obvious ones tripped off the tongue quickly like driving, walking, cycling but trying to think of 60 was quite a challenge in itself! Someone suggested skydiving – what! I thought about it for a nanosecond and thought why not, yes I can do that! I figured that doing a tandem jump the guy has a vested interest to keep you safe. If I'm going down then he is too! I hoped my heart was up to it! I thought I might book in for a medical first as my poor overweight body would not be expecting me to hurl myself out of a plane at 10,000 feet! Oh my god that's actually nearer two miles, I must have been totally mad to even consider it! When I got home I settled down to write my list of the 60 challenges I thought I could manage plus a few in reserve.

This book is all about my journey to complete the challenges. I aim to do them in the calendar year that my 60th birthday falls, that is January to December 2014. This challenge is not of course on the same scale as climbing Kilimanjaro or such like, but it is MY challenge and I hope an original one and as I can't think of one good thing about getting older it will at least prove I'm 'young at heart' if not a little mad! It also gives my family a chance to get involved with some of the challenges e.g. piggy back for a mile – but shall I be the person doing the carrying or shall I be carried? With four strapping sons I feel I should be carried but this is meant to be a challenge for me so I'll decide later. I will need photos so I appoint Pete as my official photographer. I feel I just want to achieve something which could be fun and hopefully a good laugh. I realise I might fail but I'll give it my best shot and I really love the idea of having a focus for the year rather than just drifting through it as most of us tend to do.

My actual birthday is in November when I hope to have a lovely party with all my friends and family and slip into a size 12 dress without the help of support underwear! I'm currently a size 14 and have been playing at losing weight for years but a 60th birthday party must surely be enough of an incentive to make me do it, so as well as the challenge I've set for myself I will try to take my weight more seriously and lose loads of pounds! Another reason for losing weight of course is that I don't want to be too heavy for when I'm strapped to the skydiver as psychologically I want him to hardly know I'm there, so he can give his full attention to getting us both down safely!

Fifty two weeks in a year means I have to do more than one a week, in fact I have to do five a month and it's already January 16th and I'm only just about to start! Now where to begin? Not with the easy ones I think as I'll need to keep those for when I'm losing heart. I had better get on and do this now as I can't see me being able to do this when I'm 70!

This is not meant to be a literary masterpiece. I am just a middle aged woman trying to hold on to her youth a bit by doing a fun challenge to mark her looming 60th birthday! I am looking forward to the challenges and feel really focused and confident that I can do this. They say 'life begins at 40' but right now I feel like for the first time that I'm just starting to live – I can't wait! I'm doing something just for me, I'm not being a wife or a mother, I'm being Sophie who in her head is only a young woman and certainly up for the challenge of '60 miles – my trials and smiles' (let's hope there are lots of smiles!)

Sophie Johnson.

JANUARY

20th January

Today I had my induction at a boot camp in Basingstoke which is my first step to proving that I am serious! All being well I hope to go about three times a week. I also weighed myself first thing this morning and intend to weigh myself every morning just to make sure I stay on track! I also took my measurements – bust, waist, hips, upper arms and calves and thighs. Like a lot of women I have battled with my weight for years and years, in fact I think I gained half a stone after each child! I have a little red book where I record my weight, which I started on 28th December 2004! My friend and I used to meet up once a week and weigh ourselves hoping we were down on the previous week, and if not always vowed to try harder! The worrying thing is that for years I was always half a stone lighter than her but nowadays she is actually about three quarters of a stone lighter than me! That's what having a toy boy does for you – her not me! We don't weigh together anymore because I would just get depressed and then eat to comfort myself so no point really, however I really do want to lose weight so I will try. I don't want to become a self-obsessed bore about my weight so I will just record it in this book every two weeks.

Weight: 12 stone 0.8 lbs and 42% fat!!!!!

21st January

My first boot camp session! Oh my god it was so hard and I'm dreadfully unfit. There were about 14 people in today's class, mainly women but also three men. Because I'm new I have to wear a rubber band on my wrist for the first two weeks that I go. I'm not sure if the band is to let the instructor know that I don't know what I'm doing or as a confidence booster for me so I don't feel so inadequate when I can't keep up!

I have new definitions to learn, for example burpees (complete energy sappers!) and zombies. Each class lasts for 45 minutes and when the time was up after this first session my face was absolutely blood-red, I was sweating (sorry I know ladies aren't meant to sweat but merely glow, but I tell you I was seriously sweating) and felt absolutely drained and exhausted!

On the drive home I thought about it and decided it can only get better if I stick with it. For your monthly fee you can attend as many times as you like. There are about six classes per day to fit in with people's busy lives so there are no excuses not to go! Of course the more frequently I go the easier it must get – surely! This boot camp is not like a normal gym, there are classes and you're told what to do, so no more running on a treadmill for however long you feel like as the class is very structured. In fact there is no treadmill there, this is different and I intend to give it my best shot! The trainers are all very friendly and you get a motivational email every day – not for everyone but I quite like it!

26th January

It is high time I started these challenges and today was wet and miserable so time to do my first challenge indoors somewhere. In the afternoon it brightened a little so Pete and I went to Reading station where I know they have some long escalators. I spoke to Terry (the chap on the barrier) who was happy and somewhat bemused for me to undertake my first challenge. I think he thought I was a bit mad, but as the station was quiet he was okay about it. I started going up and down while Pete busied himself working out how many circuits I would have to do to complete the mile. After a while he told me 60 escalators or 30 complete circuits. I started at 3.05pm and finished at 4.11pm. Hardly an arduous task, but good to start off with an easy one. I must admit I did feel a little self-conscious just going up and down and I was getting a couple of funny looks, but I tried not to notice! Keep them guessing – it will give them something to talk about over their dinner table tonight, the mad woman they saw who was just going up and down the escalators for fun! I found it very boring, but felt pleased to be finally making a start on these challenges.

Getting started is often the hardest part, but once you do the bug takes hold and you just want to get on with it. That's what I'm hoping anyway! The highlight was when Pete disappeared for a while to buy a coffee and returned with one for me as well which I enjoyed sipping over the next few circuits.

When I'd finished we thanked Terry, who by this time had been joined by another staff member, for letting me do this. We spent a few minutes talking to them both about the other challenges I had planned, and they both agreed the idea was great and wished me the very best of luck! That was nice of them. Perhaps this whole idea isn't so silly after all! Hurray I've actually done one – 59 to go!

Pete worked out the distance as 87.41(length of horizontal distance)x60÷3 (to give the total in yards) = 1748.2 yards which is not quite the mile, so I actually completed 31 circuits totalling 1806.47 yards which is plenty as there are 1760 yards in a mile. When we got outside it was still raining but we hadn't wasted the day and that felt good!

Cost: £4.40 car park

28th January

I phoned Rycroft Riding School in Eversley and booked a private ride through the woods being led on a lead. This is seriously brave of me as I don't feel comfortable around animals! I have booked for 6th February at 2pm. I also phoned Planet Ice in Basingstoke and one of their trainers, Rachel, is going to give me a half hour skating lesson on 4th February at 1.30pm in preparation for the mile-long skate – great stuff!

30th January

When Felix was 18 he went to Winchester University and by his own admission admits he didn't work that hard and he socialised far too much, and as a result he didn't achieve his full potential. He has matured a lot since then due to what life has thrown at him, and he now wants to give university another go. Today we went to Greenwich University open day to see what they can offer him, but despite having an open mind all three of us left feeling it just wasn't right for him. Oh well, there are lots of other universities to choose from. Felix just wants to be the same as everyone else, and everyone else it seems goes to university! His oldest brother Marcus went to Plymouth, but as with Felix he was too immature and didn't achieve his potential, although he has now found his niche in life as an estate agent. Harry went to Bournemouth and achieved a 2:2 in Business Information Systems Management (whatever that is!) and Freddie is currently in Bristol studying Property Development and Planning so I totally see where Felix is coming from – as the youngsters say!

FEBRUARY

1st February

I called into the 'Skiplex' in Basingstoke to have a look at their dry ski slope, as this is where I hope to do the ski challenge. I spoke to a nice young man called Ollie, who thought my challenge idea was brilliant. He said he will email me with details of how many times or how long I will have to stay on the slope (which moves like a conveyor belt) in order to accomplish the mile. I hope he doesn't forget!

3rd February

Weight: 11 stone 11.6 pounds and 42% fat. Total loss 3.2 lbs and I've been to boot camp 6 times. Happy with this – hope I can keep it up!

After work today Pete and I went to Absolutely Karting in Basingstoke. We were told that the distance around the track was 800 metres, which is good as I will only need to go round three times! I am booked in for this Thursday at 12 o'clock. Hopefully Felix will be able to come with us and have a go.

Cost: £20 had to pay today

4th February

Pete and I got to Planet Ice in good time ready for my half hour lesson with Rachael. The receptionist gave us a note from Rachael saying that she apologised, but she was unable to make it! She couldn't phone me because stupidly I had not left my contact details when I made the booking! Pete and I then thought – shall I book another lesson or just go for it? I decided that as I was there, I may as well just do it. I hired my skates and stepped gingerly onto the ice. I rather pathetically hung onto the side and very slowly worked my way round the rink, while Pete worked out how many circuits I would have to do. Being an engineer he worked it out exactly. Total perimeter length = 2 x end straight @ 13m = 26+2 x side straight @ 43m = 86+ circumference of circle 8.5 m radius= 2 pi r where r =8.5 = 2x3.142 x 8.5 = 53.4 total 26+86+53.4=165.4 therefore need to do 10 circuits equalling 1654m apparently! PHEW!!

There are 1609 metres in a mile. I actually did 11 circuits just to make sure! I have to admit that there was not a lot of style in my skating – lots of arm flailing and spasmodic body movements as I tried to maintain my balance! I lost it once on circuit eight when I went crashing backwards onto the ice. I bumped my head and bottom but a good thing about being a little overweight – you bounce well! Seriously though, I did feel a little shaken up, but being on my eighth circuit I was not about to stop! Several people rushed over to see if I was okay, which was nice of them. My pride was slightly dented and I felt embarrassed, but I was fine. I played it down because I just wanted to get this challenge done. Pete suggested stopping and giving up after my fall, but I'm quite a determined person, and so it wasn't an option. If truth be told though, I actually could have cried.

There is something about getting older that when you fall it seems to affect you much more than it would as a child and leaves you feeling shaken. Maybe it's because children cry, rub themselves down and just get on with it, while adults have this stiff upper lip thing and hold their feelings in a lot more. Maybe if we let our feelings out, we would recover quicker and not feel so unsettled and shaken for so long. Of course, the real reason is that we are falling from higher up and have a lot more weight than a child so we fall much heavier. It would be an interesting idea though to actually let our feelings out and have a good bawl if appropriate!

Eleven circuits were completed with me hanging onto the side the whole time. I'm ashamed to admit that I even asked young children who were also grasping on to the side to move away from the edge so I could pass. I started at 1.40pm and finished at 2.15pm so 35 minutes in all which is 15 minutes slower than walking pace! What have I learnt from this? I didn't enjoy it, the boots rubbed my ankles and I'm sure I will have big sores on them when I finally take my boots off. I'm not a natural, and have no wish to ever skate again, BUT challenge number two done!

Cost: £9.70

6th February

At 8am today I had a personal training session with Luke, one of the 'fitness experts' from my boot camp. This was included in my subscription, and oh my goodness it was so hard. I'm usually in a group, and when the instructor turns his back to me I frequently ease up on the exercise just to take a momentary breather. With 'one to one' training there was no escape! It was an hour long and at the end I was near to collapsing, but Luke said I did well so that made me feel a bit better. I know exercise must be good for me – either that or it's going to kill me – but it's just frustrating that weight goes on so easily, but it is exhausting work to shift even the smallest amount!

It's a wet and miserable day! Felix decided not to come karting with me today, as he had things he needs to do. I felt a bit nervous, but no idea why, as it should be fun. I had to complete a registration form on a computer before I started. Two other men were also going round with me. I broke the ice by telling them I would not be competition or a threat to them in any way, in fact I would be a hazard! They laughed and said, 'Not a problem!' We had a briefing just explaining the different flags and then we had the opportunity to improve our appearance with some tasteful boiler suits! I was allocated car number 16 and, after donning gloves and a helmet, I was off. We had 30 minutes on the track, which is 1640.4 feet long which equals 546.8 yards, so I needed to do four laps to complete the mile.

Seven laps later I went into the pits and Pete took over for the last 15 minutes. The two other men on the track were whizzing past me all the time. I have to say that I did quite enjoy it, although my average speed per lap was only 12.9mph! I really can't explain why I was so slow and cautious – I'm not a bit like that on the road! I think it was the fear of spinning or losing control (not a good feeling for a control freak like me!) Anyway, I would definitely do it again and try not to look like so much of a girl!

After the go-karting we rushed home for a quick bit of lunch then off to Rycroft Stables in Eversley for my second challenge of the day.

It was still raining unfortunately so I dressed accordingly, with a waterproof anorak and hood. Pete and I had trouble finding the stables and arrived a little late, but there was no problem with that. I was issued with riding boots and helmet and reassured by the very chatty woman on the reception that, despite my dislike of animals, I would be fine. I couldn't help but remember about the last time I was on a horse when I was unceremoniously thrown off! It must have been about 40 years ago now. I was with a colleague from Barclays Bank. I was badly winded and was lying on the ground gasping for air, which in itself is very frightening, and my friend John didn't do anything! When I challenged him later he said he thought I was laughing! I've never really felt comfortable around animals since – they are unpredictable and you don't know what they're thinking! Do they think? Anyway, Hannah appeared all bubbly and chatty and we went together to meet Zac who was a 12-year-old skewbald Irish pony: 16 hands tall, or should that be high?

He looked friendly enough, docile even as he was led to the platform which I used to mount him. I didn't make a hash of the mounting as I expected to, but when up on the horse's back you really do feel quite high up, but it was okay. We set off in the drizzle out of the stables and across the road to commence our walk. Hannah and Pete walked beside me as I was led on the lead for the mile down this muddy track.

The walk was for 30 minutes and it was soon all over. Although I'm not an animal lover my nerves did ease and I felt comfortable and safe.

However, I struggled to get off Zac when we arrived back at the stables, even though I had a concrete wall to stand on. I kept thinking I was going to fall off or Zac would bolt! Honestly I'm such a novice, but the good thing about these challenges is that I'm doing stuff I wouldn't choose to do. Hannah assured me we had travelled more than a mile on the pony, but she didn't know how far. It was enjoyable despite the rain. Would I do it again? No!

Cost: £39.00

One of my challenges is to drive a tank and I found out that Juniper Leisure in Romsey could arrange for me to drive or ride in a tank, so this evening I sent them an email.

10th February

I sent a text to Sarah who is my hairdresser to see if she happened to have a wheelchair I could borrow. She is lovely and one of those people who may for no reason whatsoever have a wheelchair tucked away in her garage somewhere. Well the reply came back 'yes' and she is happy to lend it to me for about an hour this Wednesday – great! She also said she has a motorised scooter; I will think about that one! While at work today, I phoned Basingstoke Aquadrome to enquire about their flumes. They have three, the 'yellow peril' being the tamest flume. Hopefully we'll be able to ride the flumes tomorrow afternoon. I need to talk to Pete. Perhaps he'll flume ride with me, as it would be nice to have company not to mention we'd both have a good laugh!

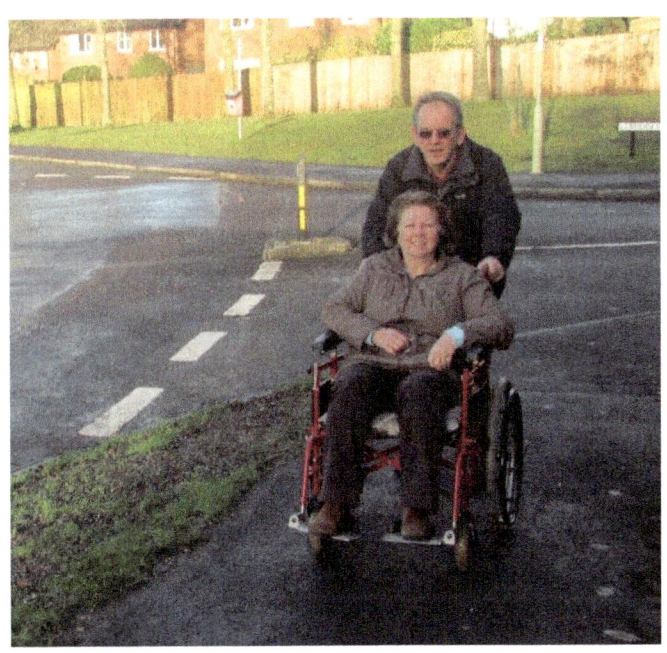

11th February

I had an email reply from Juniper Leisure in Romsey who suggested I phone them. I spoke to a lovely lady called Dorothy May. I have agreed to do the quad biking, which is an absolute bonus as I didn't even know it was an option. As for whether I go on a tank or an armoured vehicle, that will be decided when I get there. The date is booked for April 5th and the cost will be approximately £100. Great to be able to knock off another couple of challenges at the same venue.

The Aquadrome flumes are open from 4pm today. I was there changed and ready to start by 4.10pm. There were only two flumes open today: 'yellow peril' and the blue 'master blaster'. I tentatively started on the yellow peril, which is the tamest, and found it okay. I went down it twice before Pete said the blue master blaster is much longer so I wouldn't need to do as many rides. Good advice, so off I went. Pete said I needed to do the flume 22 times to complete the mile. I felt a bit scared the first time I went down the master blaster but soon got used to it. It was really good fun! Sometimes when I eventually got to the bottom I was facing backwards, but Pete never was! I've no idea why he didn't get spun round like I did; maybe he put his bottom further through the hole in the ring or something.

The Polish chap supervising at the top of the flume didn't understand why I needed to do a mile but joined in with me in counting down the 22 rides. Probably thought 'mad English woman' and left it at that. Who could argue? I would say that was a fairly fair assessment!

The hardest part without a doubt was the 71 steps I had to climb inbetween the rides while carrying a large rubber ring. I got slower and slower the more times I did it and the ring seemed to get heavier and more cumbersome. By the time I got to the top each time I was panting heavily and the expression on the Polish chap's face was like '*why*'! I looked on Google when I got home to try and establish how far

I climbed just going up the steps. Formula was: 22x71 = 1562x17 (which is the standard number of inches for most steps) = 26,554". There are 63,360" in a mile.

As I did the yellow peril twice as well it was actually 24x71 = 1704x17= 28,968" which equates to 4/9ths of a mile – that's almost half a mile! No wonder I felt so tired at the end!

I finished at 5.35pm. This challenge took me one hour and 25 minutes. Pete did about 12 flume rides and we both enjoyed it immensely, particularly as we were virtually the only ones there. It definitely brought out the child in me as I felt I wanted to squeal all the way down, although I can't speak for Pete who is far too sensible to even admit he felt the desire to squeal. It's a shame when you feel that you have to suppress the inner-child and remember that you're nearly 60 years old! I can't really see this being good fun if there had been long queues. Pete had to complete a form to be allowed to take my photo which reminds me I *must* try harder to lose weight!

Cost: £6.10

12th February

Yet again another horrible, damp, miserable day and I had to text Sarah to say that the weather was just too awful to go out in a wheelchair. Anyway, as the day progressed the rain stopped and even the sun came out, albeit only briefly. I text Sarah again to say that my wheelchair ride was back on! Pete and I drove to her house and clocked the distance in the car – it was 0.7 miles. We decided that we would go back up to our house and then back to Sarah's, a distance of 1.4 miles – perfect! So that's what we did.

I started off trying to wheel myself but it was too hard and I gave up. Pete pushed me as you can see from the photo and in my opinion I think he looks really puffed, mind you that bit was uphill! No, he's not wearing sunglasses to protect his eyes from the glimmer of sunlight we had that day, he has reactor light lenses in his ordinary glasses. I think the photo looks like a blind man pushing a woman in a wheelchair – not a good combination!

All went well until Pete almost tipped me out going up the kerb to Sarah's drive! Sarah has offered me a motorised mobility scooter for another one of my challenges – how kind of her. Another day I think. The time taken for this challenge was 32 minutes. This photo was taken by Freddie who had come home for a couple of days to play badminton. He is a very, very keen player and needs no excuses to drop what he's doing to play a game or enter a tournament!

Cost: zero!

15th February

Pete and I went to Alton Sports Centre where they have a climbing centre. We looked at the wall which is 10 metres high and watched as little kids went up with no problem at all. Could I do this? I'm not too sure. For starters I would have to go up the wall 161 times (1609 metres in a mile). At the moment it seems a very daunting challenge! Anyway, we have booked a taster session next Tuesday between 4 and 5pm before making any rash decisions. They also have a horizontal climbing wall there which we both had a little go on – not bad but somehow feels like cheating so we'll wait and see how we get on next Tuesday with the vertical one.

16th February

After so much rain it was a pleasant surprise to wake to a much brighter day. I thought I would try the crawling challenge today. I wasn't prepared to humiliate myself in public so having a reasonably large back garden I decided that it would be the perfect venue. Matthew, my next door neighbour's son, is a runner and I remembered them having a trundle wheel which was perfect for measuring out how many laps of my garden I would need to do.

So round and round I went and after fifteen and a half laps 1609 metres registered on the wheel. I decided I would do 16 laps after lunch. One huge roast dinner later and having changed into shorts and t-shirt I was ready. Pete gave me a pair of kneepads and I set off at 2.45pm.

The first lap took me about seven minutes and I couldn't believe how tired I felt. I realised that this was going to be much harder than I first thought! After each lap I had to have a drink from the bottle of water at my starting place before I could continue. This photograph shows the size of the garden which seemed to get bigger every time I went around it. My right knee pad felt uncomfortable so lap six was done wearing only the left knee pad. Lap seven was done without wearing any kneepads which by the way was a huge mistake and for laps 8 to 16 Pete had strapped great big sponges onto my knees with parcel tape! I actually finished the challenge at 4.30pm, which works out to be just under seven minutes per lap. I think I got faster but needed more rest time as I got sooooooooooooooooo tired!

I finished up with very sore knees and my left knee was now home to a very large blister. I do hope the neighbours didn't see me or I shall be expecting a knock on the door from the men in white coats to take me away, as I'm clearly mad! The way I feel right now I would think they're right! Oh, and the way Pete ripped the parcel tape off my knees means I won't need to shave them for quite a while. Did I notice a faint smile hovering on his lips? Surely not!

Cost: zero!

17th February

My weight today is 11 stone and 11 pounds. I have only lost 0.6 of a pound in the last fortnight. (Aw!!!) I have been to boot camp six times in the last fortnight, but against that I have also eaten out three days running! Life just seems to get in the way!

The problem is that I do have a life! I go out for meals, meet up with family and I'm afraid that when I go out I don't believe in dieting. It's a night out after all, so who wants to be bothered with worrying about the calorie intake? I know I don't! Also, have I mentioned that I love food? Anyway, I've loads of time yet until my party and I certainly don't want to peak too early!

18th February

As two weeks have passed since I last had contact with Skiplex I phoned them and spoke to Ollie who assures me that he did in fact send me an email straight after I visited on 1st February. Well I never received it. Funny how these things get lost in the ether somewhere! Anyway, I am now booked in for Thursday at 2pm. Apparently I need a quarter of an hour to practise and just another quarter of an hour for the challenge itself. I paid £29.99 today for the booking.

At 4pm Pete and I found ourselves at Alton Sports Centre facing the wall. We have just found out that it is not in fact 10 metres high but only 8.5 metres which means a total of 190 climbs! Martin, one of the trainers, is looking after us. We get all harnessed up and after some children in our group have had their go it's suddenly my turn. I prepare to totally embarrass myself, but to my surprise I manage to get to the top without falling off! I find it hard and taxing, but my boot camp sessions must be paying off. Although you need arm strength, it's really the legs where you need to power through. Then it's Pete's turn and of course it is now male pride at stake as his 59-year-old wife has just shot up the wall like a rat up a drainpipe (possible slight exaggeration)! I'm pleased to report that it was success for Pete as well, and he doesn't go to boot camp so he did really well! We both get a second climb and decide it is good fun, but we're both puffing and grateful that we've run out of time. We're not sure whether to continue with this challenge, as it's going to be seriously hard. I've done two climbs now so 188 to go. What am I thinking? I must be mad to even consider this!

Cost for wall taster session: £25

20th February

Pete and I turned up at Skiplex today at 1.45pm to give me plenty of time to complete my registration form and don my ski boots. There was another lady there also trying it out for the first time. Of course being February it was a busy time of year for them. There were also quite a few children with their mothers anxious for them to gain confidence before jetting off on their ski holidays. After a few minutes I was called up along with the other middle-aged woman and we clipped our skis onto our boots. We both clung on to the hand rail precariously while Emma, our teacher, switched on the conveyor belt. It's probably not called a conveyor belt, but I don't know the proper term. The bit I was standing on began to move backwards and I instantly hated it!

I was too scared to let go of the rail despite lots of encouragement from Emma, and I spent the first 15 minutes complaining like a child and lifting my hands very briefly and then quickly grabbing the rail again. It really is so hard and unnatural and when Emma started to suggest we do a snowplough I just felt like an utter failure, particularly as clever clogs next to me has taken to it like a duck to water! After 15 minutes we had to get off and let the children have a go. They were all better than me – no fear I suppose.

This photo was taken during my second 15 minute session when I must admit I was marginally better. I did fall over twice which Pete did capture on camera but thought I would put this photo in the book as you actually can't see the hand rail which is only just out of sight! This pathetic attempt was my best effort and I'm embarrassed about how bad I was. Clever clogs loved it and couldn't wait to jet off on her holiday and ski down the runs with no trouble at all. Why could she grasp it and I couldn't? I was like this with skating so perhaps I need something more thrilling and hardcore before I can really show what I am made of! Do I want to do it again? Absolutely not! I hated it, so much so that it has put me off ever wanting to go on a skiing holiday, although falling over on snow is bound to be easier than falling onto this synthetic fibrous stuff where you land quite heavily! The ramp was 30 feet long and at six miles an hour I managed to stay upright over 10 minutes. Another mile done – the worst so far!

Cost: £29.99

22nd February

Today is Freddie's 23rd birthday. It would have been nice to go and visit him in Bristol and take him out, but he's in Sheffield playing in a big tournament all weekend. As it's his birthday it would be lovely if he won but I know the standard is very high at this tournament so as long as he does his best...

23rd February

Freddie phoned last night. Apparently the tournament didn't go as well as he expected because on the Friday (the day before the big tournament) he was taken out by his friends, had a heavy night and struggled the next day to get about the court!!!! Silly boy!! Just when you think they are starting to show signs of growing up!

While Pete cooked the roast lunch I took the opportunity to walk backwards around the garden. Having already done the crawl challenge I knew I had to do 16 laps.

I started at 11.35am and finished at 12.15pm, a total of 40 minutes. It wasn't too difficult although I could feel it in my thighs. After I had finished it was strange really as I felt a bit wobbly and not quite able to maintain my balance, although the feeling did soon pass. Pete did one lap with me although he felt very silly and wasn't too keen to do more. I was quite happy as I was having my lunch cooked for me. Pete is very good like that. He certainly doesn't view cooking as solely my job. In our house one person cooks and then the other does the washing up. I think that's quite typical for most households, well it works well for us anyway.

Cost: zero!

25th February

I am feeling positive about today, because if all goes well I should get three challenges done. We are meeting up with our friends, Steve and Angie (the same Angie who came up with this crazy idea in the first place!) who live in Outwood near Bletchingley. The plan is to have some lunch at a hostelry somewhere and then Angie and I intend to do the three legged challenge. We tell them that we should get to them about 12ish so, having the morning free, Pete and I leave home much earlier than necessary. We intend to go to Gatwick Airport first to do the travelator as a challenge and the monorail, which runs between the South and North Terminals.

We parked in the Orange car park and headed to the travelator, only to find lots of Easyjet staff making some sort of promotional film. They were going up and down the travelator holding a board with a letter on which spelled out some sort of advertising slogan, if of course the staff managed to assemble themselves in the right order! They did look very smart with the look being completed with big, big smiles.

Anyway, after checking it was alright to use the travelator while they were filming, I started my challenge at 10.55am and finished at 12 o'clock. There was only one travelator going into the South Terminal so I had to keep walking back to the beginning on the concourse to the side. Pete worked out that the travelator was about 85 yards long which meant riding on it 21 times.

Of course I was not alone as a lot of passengers were also on the travelator and I'm sure it's possible that several of us will be forever preserved on some Easyjet video tape, or more likely cut out and left on the cutting room floor! It was boring just riding up and down, but at least with the filming going on it gave me something to look at and rather naughtily every time I got close to the camera I did smile. It's a sort of reaction really – you see a camera pointing at you so you smile, or is that just me?

I actually rode the travelator 22 times just to make sure I covered the mile! I was tempted to walk along the travelator but I couldn't do that because that would be walking so I just stood still and let the travelator take me! Pete took this photo after the EasyJet staff had left.

Cost: zero!

We phoned Steve and Angie to say we were going to be late and then went into the terminal to find the monorail shuttle. Pete had found out that the monorail distance between the two terminals was three quarters of a mile. Great! From the South to North Terminal and back again and all done! We got on the shuttle at 12.10pm, went to the North Terminal, which was a journey time of two minutes, waited a minute while people got off and on, and then went back again. The challenge was completed by 12.15pm. The quickest challenge ever! I look a little embarrassed in this photo as it is difficult to look normal when people around you are staring and wondering who the hell you are and why your photo is being taken! I know this photo doesn't show people staring but believe me they were! I'm trying to look 'cool' and natural but don't think I succeed!

This free monorail, which opened in July 2010, is brilliant. It took £45 million to redesign and 10 months to develop and with a running frequency of 5-7 minutes for 24 hours a day it just ticks all the boxes with regard to making travelling a less arduous experience for the travel weary passenger. It replaces the previous inter terminal shuttle which was built in 1987.

Cost for the car park: £10 for 2 hours

We arrived at our friends' house about 12.45pm and left soon afterwards to drive to Walton Heath at Mogador, which is a small hamlet on the edge of Banstead Heath. Of course Walton Heath is famous for the two 18-hole golf courses which they have there, but I suspect we won't be doing our three legged challenge there. I went with Angie in her car and Pete went with Steve. We took two cars because our destination was close to the M25 and therefore saving us going back to their house afterwards. It's always nice to catch up with friends and knew we'd have time for a good chat in the hostelry we'd be visiting!

When we arrived at the heath (not the golf club) we all put on our walking boots and prepared ourselves for the muddy trek ahead. I had recently downloaded the 'sports tracker' app to my phone so I used this to measure the distance. Angie and I tied our ankles together with Steve's scarf and set off. As the ground was uneven we did stumble quite a bit, but it was a real laugh with the ever present reality of us both falling over, which would have been really muddy after all the rain we'd had recently. It's much harder than it looks and it took us a while to get a rhythm going but we were soon in our stride and stepping it out.

It was a laugh and good fun, and that is what's nice about these challenges: you do things that you wouldn't normally do and there wasn't anyone else around so we didn't have to explain ourselves either!

We started at 1.30pm and stopped at 2pm and completed more than a mile according to my new app. We treated ourselves to lunch out at the nearby Sportsman pub and had a good old chat and catch up. We parted ways at 3.30pm as they had the school run to do. Pete drove us home with me feeling on top of these challenges – three in one day and 12 done in total, which is actually ahead of schedule! I'm feeling really positive now, perhaps this is achievable after all!

Cost: zero!

27th February

Today is the day that I have decided to do the swimming challenge. Hart Leisure Centre in Fleet has public swimming between 12 noon and 4pm. That gives me a maximum time of four hours to complete the mile. I will need to do 66 lengths as the length of the pool is 25 metres. I could just do 65 lengths as that total would be 1625 metres and to complete the mile I need to do 1609.344 metres (I know I'm a bit OCD on accuracy, but I'm determined to do these challenges properly and not cheat!) but I have a problem with stopping on an odd number so 66 lengths it will have to be! The maximum I have ever swum before is 30 lengths so I think this is going to take me a really long time. Pete however has much more confidence in me and doesn't think it will take me as long as I do. I'm there and ready to start bang on 12 o'clock as I'm sure I'm going to need the whole four hours.

After one hour I had already done 40 lengths breaststroke – I couldn't believe it – when did I get this good? I was on my own as Pete said he would come up later to take my photo as I kept on about there being no point with him getting there too early as he would just be hanging around waiting for me to finish! So I made a point of slowing down considerably otherwise I would have finished before Pete got there! When he does arrive I only have four lengths left to do. Job done! 66 lengths completed by 1.40pm. I was much, much faster than I feared.

As well as doing these challenges I have been going to boot camp three times a week which has obviously been improving my stamina a great deal. I could never have swum that fast before. I feel tired but quietly proud of how well I have done on this challenge. It was also good to have some entertainment, as there was an Aquafit class for 50 minutes going on in a different part of the pool which looked really good fun. Note to self – must join one day! Afterwards Pete and I went to a local garden centre where we had soup and a roll for lunch – lovely – followed by a stroll round the garden centre where I never fail to find something I just must have!

Cost: £4.20

MARCH

1st March

As quite a long time had passed since we went to Hawley Lake and the receptionist said that Paul would phone me, I decided to give up on them. I rang Horseshoe Lake Water Centre instead which is in Yateley. I spoke to a really helpful man called Carl who is the owner and he agreed to meet me on Wednesday after I finish work at about 4ish. He sounded great and couldn't have been more encouraging! I have a good feeling about this, and I'm confident he will do all he can to help me.

3rd March

Weight today is 11 stone 8.6 pounds. My body fat is 41%. Total loss this fortnight is 2.4 pounds! I'm quite pleased with that after my disastrous loss before of only 0.6 pounds! I believed that going to boot camp as regularly as I do now, the weight would drop off me quite dramatically, but because muscle weighs heavier than fat I am happy to console myself with that thought! It's all positive – 2.4 pounds gone, all moving in the right direction.

I feel proud that I'm sticking with the boot camp, as my fitness is definitely improving and I can certainly see that my calves have more shape. I'm feeling fairly positive and not worried yet about my weight, as there's still loads of time until November. I need to find some good exercises to tone up my upper arms just in case I want to wear a sleeveless dress at my party.

5th March

My good feeling about Horseshoe Lake was a little premature. When I phoned Carl, as he had asked me to do before visiting, he said that there were problems with the heating. Unfortunately he wouldn't be there tonight so we have rearranged for this Friday, all being well.

6th March

Pete and I went to Lasham Gliding Club today and have booked a taster session for me at 10am this Saturday. The cost will be £80. I also phoned a bike hire place at Brockenhurst Station to see if they have tandems for hire. I was pleased to hear that they do, so if the weather is favourable this weekend, I might see how many of my family I can drag along for a cycling day in the New Forest for a bit of family bonding.

7th March

We went to Horseshoe Lake to meet with Carl only to find out that he had gone home an hour ago! However, we had a useful chat with Peter who really liked my challenge idea and said that at Horseshoe Lake I could do kayaking, canoeing, sailing, pedalo and paddleboard. Fantastic! Five in one place! The lake doesn't open until April so I have left it to Peter to contact me with possible dates. I hope to hear from him next week.

8th March

Pete is a member of our local Choral Society and they rehearse every Tuesday evening. Another member called Nigel owns a Suzuki Hayabusa motorbike. Pete approached him last Tuesday about taking me out sometime this coming weekend, but not Saturday morning as I have a glider lesson booked. I have been on the back of a motorbike before but many years ago. One of my boyfriends had one and took me out, but I couldn't bring myself to lean over when we went around corners, in fact I think I leaned the other way to try to balance up the machine! You might say I wasn't a natural, but thrilling none the less!

Today is Saturday and Nigel is outside with his beast of a machine. It has a 1350cc engine and can do 0 to 60mph in just over two seconds! He lends me a helmet and I grip on around his waist for dear life! He says I can hold on to the bar at the back, but I'm not that brave. I figure that if I hold onto him it will be safer. He takes me for a ride around Rotherwick, a distance of 5.6 miles. He is very cautious and doesn't go any faster than 60mph although you can feel that there is so much more to come from the beast, but how thoughtful of Nigel to take it steady with me on the back. The reckless side of me wanted Nigel to put the beast through its paces, while I drifted back to the carefree days of my youth when speed was so exciting and we gave little thought to our safety. When you're young you don't really see the danger and, if you can, it just adds to the excitement. Nowadays with all the health and safety laws we are all so protected that I can't help thinking that we are losing the ability to be responsible for ourselves!

I thoroughly enjoyed the ride for the experience but if I'm honest I'm more of a car sort of girl!

Cost: zero!

At 10am this morning I was due for my taster gliding session at Lasham Airfield which is near Alton. They phoned to say that visibility was poor and my taster session was moved back to 3pm, so that's how come I managed to do my motorbike challenge. Pete had phoned Nigel and said that the morning was now free.

I will tell you a little bit of history about Lasham…

The village and airfield are now usually known as 'Lash-am', but until recent times most locals called it 'Lass-ham'. The village dates back to the eleventh century when it was 'Esseham', becoming 'Lessham' shortly after. The airfield was built by Irish labourers and Italian prisoners of war, and completed in 1942. Several different types of aircraft were based at Lasham during World War Two. The squadrons based at Lasham during the period 1942-44 were:

33	Spitfire
107	Boston/Mosquito
175	Hurricane/Typhoon
181	Typhoon
182	Typhoon
183 Gold Coast	Typhoon
239	Mustang
305 PAF	Mitchell/Mosquito

320 RDNA	Mitchell
412 RCAF	Spitfire
453	Spitfire
602	Spitfire (City of Glasgow)
609	Typhoon (West Riding)
613	Mosquito (City of Manchester)

During the war, cities, counties and other major groups, such as London Borough, were encouraged to raise money to directly assist the war effort by buying an aeroplane. Raising £5,000 paid for a Spitfire, and £20,000 bought a bomber. They were often called 'Spitfire Funds'. The locality would take pride in their efforts, and their name would be painted on the aircraft. 'City of Glasgow' is an example.

One of the most famous operations was by 613 Squadron. On 14th April 1944 six Mosquitos led by Wing Commander Bateson bombed the Central Records Registry of the Gestapo in The Hague from a height of 50 feet. The accuracy was such that there were few civilian casualties. Most of the buildings at Lasham Airfield from World War Two have now been demolished, except for the large hangars.

Lasham Gliding Society is now one of the largest gliding clubs in the world. Over 220 gliders are based at the airfield. The airfield is in constant use throughout the year, and regularly hosts national and regional gliding championships.

In 1999 Lasham Gliding Society (LGS) completed the purchase of the freehold of the airfield from the Ministry of Defence, making the final payment in 2001.

Anyway, moving on – I thought it wise not to have too much for lunch. Not that I'd be doing acrobatics or anything in the sky, but just in case. We got there in good time and I met my pilot, Ian, who has 40 years of experience, so I felt greatly reassured. He gave me lots of information on safety which was good, and instructions on things and instruments I mustn't touch. I didn't realise I would have to wear a parachute, and I made sure I listened very intently as he told me how to deploy it! I also didn't realise that the pilot of the glider sits at the back so I had a brilliant view from the front!

The nose of the glider was attached to a cable, which was then hooked on to a small plane. Very soon we were bumping over the ground and before we knew it we were airborne. I don't know how high the tow plane has to be before the cable is released, but I was suddenly aware that we were totally on our own with no tow plane in sight. We glided around for about 15 minutes. The weather was a bit hazy but we could see Alton and Four Marks below. I could talk to Ian and he pointed out a few points of interest, but the best bit for me was the silence. A very surreal experience – in the sky with no engine to hold you up there, and the only sound was the wind over the wings. There were unfortunately no thermals that day, so we slowly drifted back to earth having covered a distance of about 12 miles at 45mph. We landed a fair distance from where we started so a support vehicle towed us back and I had to hold the wing all the way to stop it hitting the ground.

I must say, it was a very good experience and another challenge done. Would I do it again? I don't think so, far too much faffing around! Ian was lovely though and couldn't have been nicer! I have a certificate to prove I've done it so that's the main thing!

Cost: £80

9th March

This afternoon we have been treated with a visit from the sun, and after all the rain we've had it is very welcome. Pete suggested to me a while ago that the easier challenges I should try to make more interesting by not doing them in the obvious way, but a variation. I remembered a few years ago Pete and I hired bikes from 'Country Lanes' who are a bike hire company based at Brockenhurst Station. I gave them a ring and asked if they had tandems available for hire today, or whether they had already been booked? Far more interesting than an ordinary bike I thought! Yes, they had tandems for hire today, so along with Harry, Marcus, and Isabell who is Marcus's girlfriend, we drove to Brockenhurst Station to collect one tandem and three ordinary bikes. We were given helmets, a map and a puncture repair kit before being let loose in the New Forest. We had a lovely afternoon cycling through the forest having goes in turn riding the tandem, although most of the time I was on the back as it was so low and I'm the shortest!

The disadvantage is that you can't see where you're going, but the advantage is that you don't have to worry about anything except pedalling as you don't have any brakes or gears. We picked up the bikes about 2.30pm and returned them at 4.15pm having cycled about six to seven miles. We know that because we were given maps with routes, and the distances we could work out when back at the start with the help of the bike hire company. A good afternoon and challenge 16 done!

Cost: Tandem £19, bikes x 3 = £30 therefore total was £49.00

11th of March

I had a phone call today from Peter at Horseshoe Lake who wanted to get the dates booked for the five challenges that I hope to do there. We have booked kayaking, canoeing and paddleboard for Tuesday, 15th April and sailing and pedalo for Thursday the 17th April. The cost is £18 which I have paid today online.

17th March

My weight today is 11 stone 9.8 pounds! Body fat is 40.5%. Unfortunately that is an increase in weight of 1.2 pounds, although half a percent lower in body fat. I am still going to boot camp two or three times a week but I do eat out quite a lot being a lady who lunches. I look through the menu and say to my friend, 'Let's have a decent main course then we won't need a pudding.' We both agree that's a good plan. Anyway, we don't know what the available puddings are yet, as they tend to be on a different menu. The waitress cunningly hides it from us until the appropriate time, when she suddenly pounces and lures us in with goodies such as Eton Mess! She's no fool! My resolve just disappears and I play my next game which is I can have the pudding because I won't have any tea tonight! I hope someone reading this can identify with me, or am I alone?

Still loads of time until November, so I think that may be part of the problem – no need to panic yet.

I'm not yet reaching for the chocolate in total despair! Although I do know that I eat too much, the problem is simply that I just love food and I'm weak!

Pete and I called into Blackbushe Airport today to enquire about a helicopter flight.

We were told a 15 minute flight would be £110. I thought that sounded quite a lot so I said I would think about it. In the evening I looked online and found 'Adventure 001'. They will do a five minute flight for £29 covering a distance of six miles – perfect! I have booked and paid for two tickets, I might as well give Pete a little treat as well as me! Date booked Sunday 11th of May.

27th March

When I got home from boot camp, the weather looked reasonably settled and I thought that now would be a good time to skip round the garden. Having to do five challenges per month means that I have to keep the pressure on myself, and it's now been two and a half weeks since my previous challenge. Well here I am! I started at 11.48am and finished at 12.25pm having completed 16 laps. I could have used a skipping rope but I fear that would have been even harder so I just 'skipped' round. It was far more tiring than I expected – I don't think I have fully recovered from boot camp which I went to this morning. Pete did a couple of laps with me, as did Felix. I haven't skipped once since I was about eight years old when I had endless energy and weighed the same as a feather. Nowadays it is very different! We had a real laugh as we knew we looked completely daft! Seeing this photograph is a shock reminder that I need a note to self – I must try harder to lose weight!

To be fair though, still wearing the lycra leggings I wore to boot camp isn't doing me any favours!

Freddie is home from university tomorrow, staying just for the weekend to do an interview he needs for his dissertation, and this weekend is also Mothering Sunday, so I expect we'll eat out again – what's a girl to do?

29th March

A nice and easy challenge today! It is the Saturday before Mothering Sunday and Pete and I are off to Highcliffe so we can leave some flowers for my mum and then meet Dad for lunch. After a huge carvery (aargh!!!) we drove to Hengistbury Head which is a nature reserve on a scenic headland near Bournemouth.

It is well known for its various habitats – heathland, grassland, scrub, woodland, freshwater wetland and coastline. It attracts many visitors every year, and school trips often come here to study the cliffs from which its dramatic history can be seen. The layers of sands, gravels and clays that make up Hengistbury Head were formed around 65 million years ago beneath a warm tropical sea. This was the beginning of a very unstable period. Movements in the earth's crust created The Alps but in southern England the land surface was gently folded. Temperatures and sea levels fluctuated widely. Tropical seas gave way to warm lagoons followed by extreme cold as a series of ice ages gripped the land.

I remember all four of my boys coming here with the school to study the cliffs and then having to do a project on their findings.

From near the car park you can ride the land train down to the spit, which is a journey of one and a half miles as illustrated in the next photo.

The spit is home to more than 300 privately owned beach huts which are rented out for up to £600 per week in the high season. One beach hut in 2012 became the UK's most expensive, by selling for an unbelievable price of £170,000 just two days after being put on the market! The hut measures just over 5x3 metres and has no running water!

After riding the land train Dad, Pete and I walked along the spit and took some photos on the beach. Dad gave me some photography tips (a bit of a standing joke, my lack of knowledge!) and then we strolled back up the spit to wait for the next train returning to the car park. A surprising number of people around, I guess they were all enjoying the sunshine like us. The train journey was about 10 minutes or so. A lovely way to spend a warm March afternoon!

Cost: £9.00 (Dad's treat)

31st March

Weight: 11 stone 8.4 pounds. My fat is 40%. Hooray I'm down 1.4 pounds!!! I do hope I can build on this and not slide up again. It is a very small loss but it is a loss, so I must try and be heartened by this – if I can lose about 1.5 pounds every fortnight then by November I will be 24 pounds lighter which equates to my weight being under 10 stone! BRING IT ON!

APRIL

2nd April

For some time now Felix has been on to me about joining my boot camp. With his history of brain haemorrhage, naturally I was not keen but I was equally determined he should live his life as normally as possible. He had seen how much pleasure I derived from it and how much fitter and healthier I felt. It's a funny thing about exercise, as not only do you feel better physically it also affects your mood and confidence. I'm not sure why it should, but it definitely seems to. Anyway, I had to agree as long as he promised me he would take it easy and not push himself too hard. So today Felix has his induction with James. It is only about 20 minutes long and you do a few exercises but not too much at all. It's more about what you hope to achieve, and the importance of commitment to reach your goals. The instructors encourage you to attend three times a week and work at your personal best and don't worry about what the other boot campers are doing.

Felix loved it and was now officially on his 10 day free trial. He can't wait to get started so we are booked in for tomorrow for his first proper boot camp and serious exercise in a very long time!

3rd April

Felix and I went to boot camp at 10am this morning. It was exhausting!! Even after the warm up Felix and I both agreed that we were ready to go home now! We stuck with it, albeit at our own pace and after 45 minutes it was all over. We were both sweating like mad and had beetroot coloured faces, and I do mean literally beetroot coloured! There was a sort of smug satisfaction that descended upon us on the way home as we looked at everyone else and knew that they hadn't worked as hard as we had. How good did we feel! Felix did so well and gave it his all so you can't ask more than that now can you? We decided to leave it a couple of days before going again to give our aching muscles a chance to recover.

5th April

We are off to Juniper Leisure today near Winchester for two more challenges. The weather is looking fairly miserable, and as I hope to ride a tank and go on a quad bike, I'm expecting to get wet and muddy!

Pete and I arrived in good time and were given a briefing along with others who were there for the day. Everyone was in good spirits and the members of staff seemed to be really lovely and helpful. I was issued with a purple vest to differentiate me from the others – probably to warn the instructors that I'm the 'mad one'! It's the quad bike first. It is a Honda Fourtrax 250 with a 229cc 4 stroke engine and a 5 speed gear box. I got kitted up with gloves, balaclava, helmet and goggles and then I was ready to go.

The instructors gave us a lesson in how the quad bike worked and then we were all taken to a small circuit to get a feel for it, before being let loose on the course! I don't know why, but I felt surprisingly nervous and hesitant to the point where I actually said to Pete that I wanted to go home! Pathetic, honestly! Pete wisely said I'd be fine, and that I always get like this when I'm slightly out of my 'comfort zone' and once I've dipped my toe in the water I am always okay, and in fact, often end up loving whatever it is that I am so scared of!

The two instructors Jason and Andy promised to look after me and this photograph shows Andy right on my tail keeping close, just to make sure I was okay. The quality of the photograph is not good as it had started to drizzle with rain and a light mist had descended. I was still on the small circuit at this point, but Andy's presence was reassuring to me, and as I went round a few times I gained confidence that I was not about to fall off, so I started to relax and thought 'yes, I can do this'.

After the instructors were happy with us all, we were allowed onto the main course and set off at speed (I was the slowest and at the back) over some rough terrain for about a quarter of an hour's ride. Some of the terrain was just rough tracks which wasn't too difficult at all. Further on though there was some manoeuvring to do as we went through a wooded area with big dips full of mud, which we had to ride through, and then negotiate the tree stumps at the other side which, if taken at too much speed, I guess could flip you over. As every minute passed I gained in confidence and was soon riding through the dips as confidently as everyone else and I got just as muddy.

It was really good fun – I managed a couple of tail spins which made me feel I was keeping up with the boys but all too soon we were back at the start, our quarter of an hour over. I think my maximum speed was about 30 kph. I know that's not fast but it certainly seemed fast to me! Andy and Jason said I had definitely covered the mile but I'm unsure exactly how far I went but as long as the mile is done I'm happy!

Cost £30.00

Kevin is in charge of the Chieftain MBT. It weighs 55 tonnes and is powered by a 750 hp British Leyland L60, which is a 19 litre, 6 cylinder, super-charged, compression ignition, multi-fuel 2 stroke engine – wow! It was a development on the legendary Centurion and had a much better cross-country speed. There were 2280 built in total and it was the UK's main battle tank of the 1960s, 1970s and 1980s. When it was introduced in 1966 it had the most powerful main gun and most effective armour of any tank in the world. It remained in service until replaced by Challenger 1. Four hundred and twenty Challenger 1s were produced through the 1990s then followed by the Challenger 2 which remains the standard British Army battle tank of today.

Unfortunately I hadn't paid to drive the tank but my challenge was to travel a mile in 60 different ways so riding on the top of the tank does still qualify as a mode of travel. There are places to stand on the top of the tank with hand rails to hold onto which you can see in the photograph.

The weather was very drizzly now, and you can see where the rain had dropped onto the lens of the camera. The ride on the tank consisted of going up and down a muddy track which Pete calculated that for me to do the mile I would have to travel up and down six times. Some of the other people in my group had paid to drive the tank so one person drove up and down and then swapped with the next driver and so on. I stayed on while six different drivers had their turn at driving. Of course there was no room for the tank to turn round so when it reached the end of the track the novice driver then had to reverse it all the way back to the start – quite challenging I thought as they were all first time tank drivers! This photograph was taken after all the other drivers had got off and I asked if I could stand in the driving space to have my photo taken.

Before coming home Pete and I enjoyed an egg and bacon roll and a hot drink. They gave me a certificate – job done! Juniper Leisure Staff were great!

Cost: £20

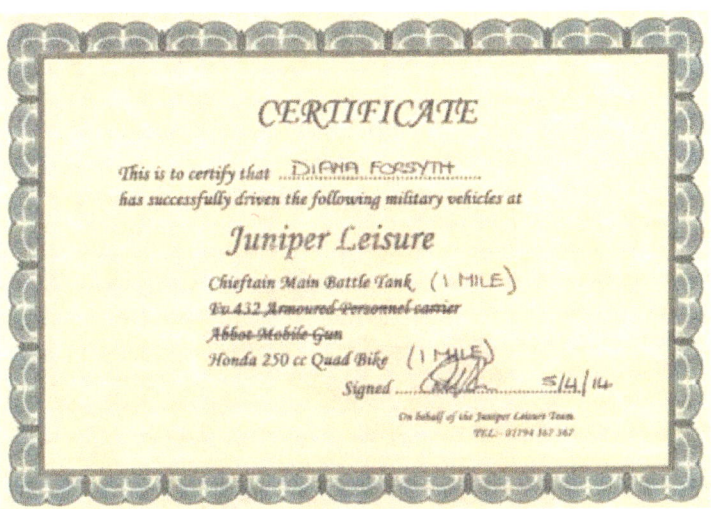

12th April

During the week I had sent a text to Sarah to see if I could borrow her mobility scooter for this Saturday. Well here we are – Pete cycled down from our house and I drove. This photograph shows Sarah her husband Steve and me getting ready for the off.

They acquired the scooter when Steve had a nasty motorbike accident and was unable to drive for a long while, so this scooter provided some freedom for him and some degree of independence. The scooter or rather mobility bike is called a Pride Mobility XL 8 Legend. I think the top speed is 8mph.

I set off at 10.05am and completed the challenge at 10.20am. I rode the scooter exactly the same route as I did when I did the wheelchair challenge. The route was up through our housing estate to Sarah's road at the top and then back again. There was one embarrassing moment when I passed a neighbour of ours who unfortunately has to use a mobility scooter for real. She was coming down the road as I was going up. She sort of did a 'double take' when she saw me and said, 'Hello,' and I flippantly said, 'Don't ask.' Why I said that I've no idea, as I could just have easily stopped and talked to her for a while and explained what I was doing. It really was embarrassing! I felt sort of awkward because she has to use a mobility scooter to get about and I was using one for fun. It felt wrong, which is why I think I behaved in such a flippant manner. She is good friends with Kath my next door neighbour, and I've since heard that she has asked Kath if I am okay, as she was so shocked to see me in a scooter and not zipping along the road as I normally do! Kath kindly explained about my challenges – so that's now another person who has me down as mad!

Cost: zero!

14th April

Weight today is 11 stone 7.2 pounds with 40% body fat. Weight loss is 1.2 pounds in the last fortnight. I know I was aiming for 1.5 pounds so already I've slipped, but at least I have lost *some*, so slow and steady is the way as fast and furious doesn't work as the weight just piles on again as soon as you take your eye off the ball!

15th April

We woke to an absolutely beautiful spring day. Pete and I were off to Horseshoe Lake Water Sports Centre for 10am ready to do three of my five challenges. Canoeing, kayaking and paddleboard today and sailing and pedalo on Thursday. We met up with Peter Ricketts who kitted us out with wetsuits, life jackets and helmets. The circumference of Horseshoe Lake is about 1km so Pete and I decided that if we went round twice on each activity we would definitely cover the mile. We set off and tried to stay as close to the edge as we reasonably could without impaling ourselves in a tree! It was so calm and peaceful. We started with canoeing and had one oar each, but because I am not a natural at rowing, instead of us each rowing one side each which resulted in us going round in circles we had to both row on the same side and then both swap to the other side to level ourselves up! We

didn't quite have the lake to ourselves but very nearly. We completed this challenge in 35 minutes. There is something about being on water, life seems to slow down and no one rushes. It felt quite idyllic! That suits me just fine as life seems so frantic and pressured so much of the time.

Doing these challenges is making me do things I wouldn't normally do, which is great. I've always known about this lake but never had the thought upon waking to a beautiful day that we must go up there and have a day 'messing about on water' but I might now!

The next challenge was kayaking. Pete and I had a kayak each, and Pete gave me some instructions while at the lake's edge about how to use the paddle which made me feel confident that I could do this. What false confidence that was! It felt very unstable as I got in and it was wobbling about all over the place; I just had a feeling that this was only going one way and that's with me taking a dip!

As soon as I got out into open water and away from Pete's help I found that I was just going round in circles and it was not as easy as I thought! I honestly don't know what I was doing wrong but it was as if my left arm is much weaker than my right. I was completely uncoordinated and had to paddle one side at a time to make any progress at all, and particularly to keep going straight!

Three quarters of the way round the first lap and for no reason whatsoever that I could see, I totally capsized and fell headlong into the lake! Imagine fishing with your mouth – that was me! Thankfully due to the wetsuit the cold did not overwhelm me, in fact it was sort of funny and fortunately it wasn't captured on film so my blushes were spared, but I could certainly appreciate how funny I must have looked.

Pete paddled over and he had the sense to not laugh at me but I'm sure he must have wanted to really. I handed him my paddle while I struggled to haul my bulk back into the kayak. It took quite a bit of effort but thankfully, partly due to boot camp and a dogged determination, I managed it and we set off again. The second lap was completed without further mishap. We started this challenge at 11:50am and completed it at 12:45pm so the duration of this challenge was 55 minutes. I think that if I had managed to master the paddle and do it properly this could well be the perfect way to while away an hour or two on a lovely summer's day. The idea is for the only sound to be the oars breaking the water for company. Well, that's how it should be according to the text books although I know different!

Now for the challenge I've been dreading – paddleboard. This is basically just a surfboard with fins underneath. The idea is to stand on the board, feet apart, with one foot further forward than the other and then paddle alternate sides to plough through the water. Reality of course is nothing like that: for a start I was kneeling down and because of that the paddle was far too long for me to manoeuvre from side to side, so I did a couple of strokes on the right and a couple of strokes on the left. Very slow progress but I was moving (a little) so I was happy. I started to get a bit more confident and actually managed to kneel up which was much better and not so uncomfortable.

I was completely on my own as Pete in his capacity as official photographer was walking along the footpath around the lake's circumference to keep an eye on me and to take some photos when he could get close enough to the edge of the lake. With my confidence soaring I started to feel a bit cocky and thought I could stand up and do it properly – mistake! I told Pete what I was planning on doing so he switched the camera to video and told me he was ready when I was. I was very careful but not careful enough, as I tumbled headlong into the lake which Pete did manage to catch on video, though it's a bit jerky as he was laughing so much! I started laughing as well as I knew how funny it must've looked! Fortunately the paddle was fastened to my ankle by a long strap so at least I didn't have to worry about that as I hauled myself back onto the board.

I continued the rest of my lap kneeling up and stayed in that position until three quarters of the way round the second lap. Being a determined little thing, I tried for a second attempt at standing. Possibly a little better – I certainly got both feet flat on the board, it was just the standing upright which proved difficult. So again I got up close and personal with the lake for the second time on this challenge and the third time today. It was funny but I know when I'm beaten and a natural paddle boarder I'm not! I really struggled to get back on to the board but finally managed it on my third attempt! I was seriously tired by now and suffering from a lack of energy. I paddled back to the shore – challenge done – I was exhausted! I started at 1pm and finished at 2:05pm.

Three challenges done today so I feel really pleased, but right this minute I'm ready for hot bath and a hot chocolate with cream and marshmallows as I feel I really deserve it!

17th April

Pete and I are back at Horseshoe Lake today for the pedalo and sailing challenge. The weather is glorious and surprisingly warm for April which is typically the month for showers, but not today. I am hopeful that today will be a lot easier than the Tuesday just gone. The idea is that we join the sailing class for a bit of tuition before the challenge itself. When we get there however, we are told that the sailing will have to be later as there is no wind! Obviously that is a necessity so later it is.

We therefore decided to do the pedalo challenge first. Peter told us that wetsuits would not be necessary as it is virtually impossible to upturn a pedalo but he did insist we wore life jackets. The pedalo was a four seater and definitely meant for four people which we soon realised after we started. It was so hard! We had to sit in the rear two seats so Pete could steer us with the tiller. Neither of us could believe how much effort we had to put in as we inched our way around the lake. The steering was very slow to respond and I kept nagging Pete to go closer to the bank, as I had to ensure a mile was covered. There was to be no cutting corners on my watch!

The first lap took us 35 minutes which included frequent stops to give our quadriceps a rest. We found that if we left off the pedals for long we started to drift into the bushes or even backwards which was no help whatsoever! The second lap took us 45 minutes which is ages for such a short distance. You know when your legs are tired and you push down on your thighs to make them work? Well virtually the whole second lap was done like that! It felt more like an endurance test than a pleasure! Added to that it was also very physically tiring with regard to breathing and stamina and with Pete being 65 I felt it only right to keep stopping and give him a chance to rest! Yeah yeah!

The photograph was taken by Peter and I'll let you guess as to whether it was taken at the start or the end of the challenge!

The wind picked up more so the sailing was definitely on. Pete and I went to our respective changing rooms and shortly reappeared in wetsuits and helmets. Along with a young girl Isabel we were given a short briefing by Charlie (a girl) who explained a triangular route we could sail between three buoys. We would have to zigzag to catch the wind. I must confess that I was not really listening as Pete has sailed before many times and was obviously in charge. He stressed to me that I must do as he told me on the boat. Funny, that sentence is normally thought (if not said) by me to him but without 'the boat'! I agreed and hoped he wouldn't become too bossy! Charlie took us to the boat and expressed concern about the size of it in relation to Pete, who is six foot one. She showed me where to sit and reminded me to watch out for the boom which would swing back and forth as the wind direction changed. After the pedalo challenge I was more than happy to sit and do nothing, so all the pressure was on Pete. We set off at 11:30am and planned to do four triangular circuits which would easily be a mile or more.

So there we were, zigzagging along with the boat rocking gently with the wind, when suddenly I was sharply aware of being very close to the water and the boat almost on its side. I shouted to Pete to see if he wanted me to move to the other side of the boat to distribute the weight, but the reply came back, 'No you're fine.' Then for the first time that day but the fourth time in two days I was again propelled headlong into the freezing water, and came to the surface coughing and spluttering! I was not happy! Charlie the instructor, who was also on the lake in the safety boat teaching Isabel sailing techniques, sped over in her speedboat to ask what happened. I assured her I was okay and Pete gallantly helped me to clamber aboard again which was the least he could do! My technique for clambering aboard was with a motion like a moving caterpillar with my middle bit rising up-and-down – not a pretty sight!

I got back in position and was waiting for an apology from Pete which did not come! I sulked and could not bring myself to talk to him, so as well as the silence of the lake we had silence on the boat also! Eventually I said, 'I think you should have apologised,' only to be told it was the wind's fault and not his! Oh that's alright then!

The challenge took us 55 minutes and when it was over we went back to the changing rooms to get changed into our clothes. Wetsuits by the way are extremely difficult to get on and off, but absolutely essential if you, like me, lake swim four times in two days! To warm up we had two muffins each with tea and hot chocolate. When we left Peter was nowhere to be seen. I left Charlie my email address so she could email me the details of the five vessels I went on so I could record them in my journal. Peter only charged me £18 for these five challenges – amazing value! Though I never did receive the information I wanted!

Cost: £18

28th April

Weight today is 11 stone 7.6 pounds which is an increase of 0.4 pounds! Body fat is 40.5 %. That was not meant to happen! In my defence I have been to a party and had to endure Easter with all that yummy chocolate lying around! Pete bought me a great big Cadbury's Easter egg (how very cruel of him!) and as much as I knew I shouldn't eat it, it would have been unkind of me to refuse his gift, so being the dutiful wife that I am I forced it down so as not to hurt his feelings! How noble am I? I'm not going to panic as I feel my weight is still under control – it's just a tiny blip and an increase of 0.4 pounds is so negligible it's hardly worth mentioning at all!

MAY

3rd May

Today Pete, Dad and I are setting off on holiday! We are going on a one week cruise down the River Rhine on a boat called the 'Swiss Tiara' organised by Riviera Travel. It's a very slow paced holiday but sometimes it is good to slow down and 'smell the flowers' as the expression goes. Also, my dad is 88 and unfortunately past the days of high activity and being on the go all the time (not sure he ever was actually!) This way he gets a lovely holiday with Pete and me to keep him company. Don't get me wrong, we'll really enjoy it as well, which I know because last year the three of us went down the Danube. It was a different travel company but excellent all the same.

Dad came to stay with us the night before so we wouldn't be so rushed. Our flight from Gatwick to Basal left at 1ish so we had comfortable time in the morning for last minute decisions about what to take. The trouble with holidaying in early May is knowing what to take. It's not quite full summer garb but it's not winter either – I guess it is layers then!

We arrived at Gatwick and got parked up, then proceeded through security, found a café and settled down with a coffee and cake. (The over-eating has officially started as I wouldn't normally have a cake with my coffee!) I wandered off to buy a magazine and sweets for the flight. When I returned to Dad and Pete I was shocked to realise just how much time had passed. It was now only 30 minutes before the flight was due to leave!

Pete and I are okay sprinting through airports but my poor dad, although in great shape, has left his sprinting days well and truly behind! We decided that I would run ahead and tell the staff at check-in that the other two in my party were on their way. I just couldn't believe just how far away our gate was – it was miles! Well not actually miles but a very, very long way! It must have been the furthest gate from the departures lounge in the whole of Gatwick! My poor dad was exhausted by the time he reached the gate but we were in time thankfully, and as he'd done so well, the least we could do was let him sit by the window! I did feel guilty as it was my fault but I've been forgiven now and anyway, age shouldn't be a barrier to older people doing exercise, it just shouldn't be that intensive for that long – oh well! On the plus side his heart must be strong! The flight passed without incident and one hour and 35 minutes later we touched down in Basal.

I sat in my seat as everyone left the plane and when I was the only passenger left I got up and Pete snapped my photo. I only needed to do one mile on a plane but did 425 – that's another challenge done!

Basal airport is amazing as there are three exits all for different countries! You can leave the airport and be in France, Switzerland or Italy depending on which exit you take – I love that! We met our cruise ship courier and left by the exit that took us to Switzerland.

Cost: zero (I know the flight was not zero but we would pay this anyway as it's a holiday so I'm counting cost of challenge as zero)

6th May

We were all enjoying the river cruise very much and the weather had been kind to us. Not so kind were the chefs who every day tempted us with delicious looking food, it really was superb and there was plenty of it. There may not have been masses on the plate but after five courses believe me you leave feeling totally satisfied! I weighed myself the day we left and I weighed 11 stone and 7.8 pounds. I know I am not strong enough to say no to any food that is just put in front of me, especially when it is so beautifully presented. I'm on holiday so that's okay isn't it? Don't we all play that game? I tell myself that I'll go to boot camp every day for a while after we get back.

All of the excursions were included and we all thoroughly enjoyed going to Lucerne and Interlaken on day two. On day three we visited Lake Titisee and the Black Forest and on day four the excursion was to Strasbourg, where we decided to look around the cathedral. This is a fine example of late Gothic architecture. It is the sixth tallest church in the world and the highest still standing structure built entirely in the Middle Ages.

It was completed in 1439 and being made from red sandstone gives the cathedral its characteristic pink hue. The cathedral has one single, tall spire which has become a symbol for the proud city of Strasbourg.

We deposited Dad in the pews for a rest while Pete and I climbed the steps to the platform of the cathedral tower to enjoy the views of Strasbourg. We started at 1.20pm and reached the top at 1.26pm. It was a height of 66 metres and a total of 330 steps. I'm a boot camper so was confident this would be a breeze! In this photo however I am looking very red-faced from all the exertion but still smiling – I think Pete took it when I was nearing the top, well I must have been, so that's excusable then as anyone would be a bit red faced after 330 steps!

I had to stop three or four times on the way up to catch my breath but I got to thinking that maybe climbing steps could be another idea for a challenge? My dad reckons it would be a very hard challenge, particularly if I want all the steps to be in a church, or preferably cathedrals, which I think I do! The number of metres in a mile is 1610 and we have just done 66 metres in six minutes so I think this might be a possible challenge as I still have seven months to complete it.

There was not a lift to get down but a different set of steps, so at least we did not have to negotiate around people, which is always a bit precarious on spiral steps! Back down on the ground Pete and I thought that this challenge of climbing steps was doable, but to make it more challenging we will try and ensure the buildings are all cathedrals. Of course if they were all different cathedrals that would be perfect but totally impractical, as I would have to spend the rest of the year travelling the country to get the job done. Even then we would probably fail as with our health and safety laws we probably wouldn't be allowed up on our own, and would have to join a tour every time! This challenge is beginning to sound ridiculously hard but I'm prepared to give it a go and see how it works out! Only 1544 metres to go!

Cost: €5 each

7th May

The excursion for today takes us to Speyer where there is another cathedral which is a fine example of Romanesque architecture. It was opened in 1106 and is one of the most important Romanesque monuments from the time of the Holy Roman Empire. It was the burial place of German Emperors for almost 300 years. It has four towers and two domes, and Pete and I are going to climb one of the towers.

Again poor Dad is left alone, after being assured by me that we won't be long. The climb is 304 steps and 60 metres and as you can see from the photo the steps have grip underfoot which is a good idea, as in this cathedral we have to go down the same way as we go up and have to pass other people. It took us 15 minutes to climb to the top but we did keep stopping to admire the view and catch our breath of course. We have to remember that we're not as young as we were! Coming down only took us four minutes though!

I notice in this photograph a 'first aid point' and I wonder what that red box is? I guess it must be a defibrillator or something for those non boot campers for whom the climb is just too much! It was a lovely

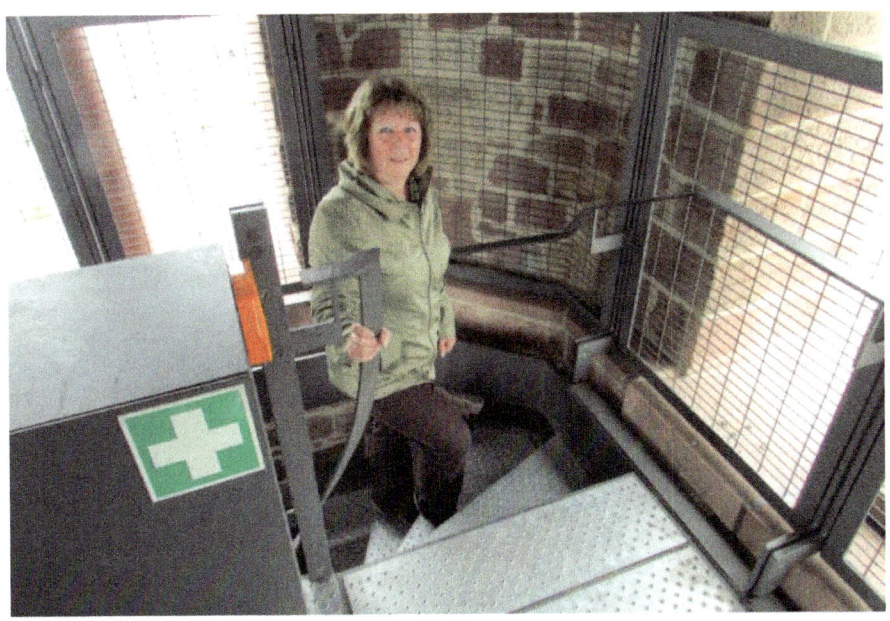

clear day and we got a really good view over the town when we got to the top.

It was well worth the climb but more importantly 60 more metres done! 1484 metres to go!

Cost: €6 each.

8th May

Today we found ourselves in Rudesheim, which is a charming wine town on the edge of the Rhine gorge and part of the UNESCO world heritage site. From here you can get a cable car up to the Niederwald Monument. It commemorates Germany's victory over France in the 1870/1871 war, and at the same time the unification of Germany, which had previously consisted of a collection of several smaller states and principalities. The construction work took six years and the monument was finally inaugurated in 1877. On top of the monument stands the imposing statue of Germania who, since Roman times, had served as a personification of Germany. This stern maid stands watch on the Rhine ready to ward of potential invaders. This particular Germania is around 10.5 metres (33 foot) high and weighs 12 tons.

The most famous attraction in Rudesheim is the Drosselgasse, which is a lane in the heart of Rudesheim's old town, full of beautifully decorated restaurants. Live music plays throughout the summer in the many wine taverns and open-air garden taverns along the 144-metre-long narrow, cobblestone pedestrian street. Built in the 15th century, the Drosselgasse was for boat owners to move items from the river to homes in the town.

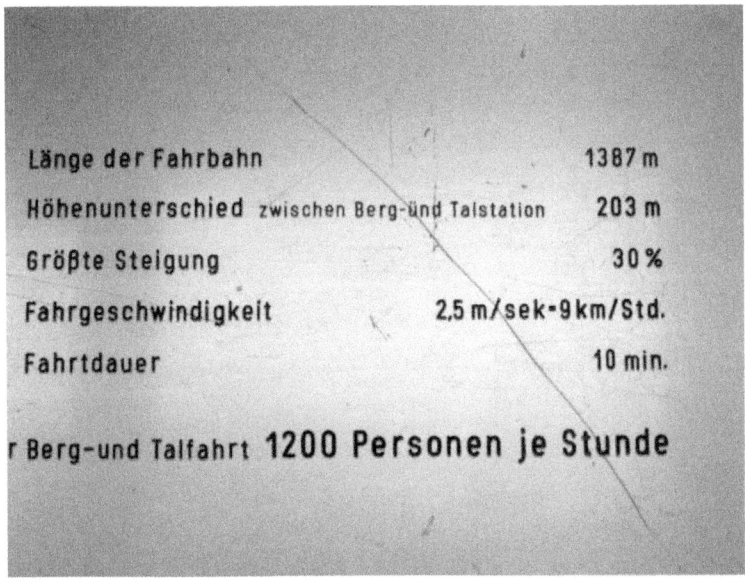

As you can see from this photo the cable car ride is 1387 metres long so one journey up and down will result in another mile completed. I handed my camera to Pete who got in the cable car behind the one

Dad and I travelled in so he could get a good shot of me doing the challenge. I settled down with Dad to enjoy the ride and the views of the vineyards and the Rhine River as we peacefully glided along enjoying the quietness away from the town. It was a lovely day with few people about, so it was like the whole cable car experience was running just for us!

Cost: €7 each.

9th May

The last stop before we headed home was Cologne. The construction of the Gothic cathedral was started in 1248 and halted in 1473. The construction was restarted in the nineteenth century and the cathedral was finally opened in 1880. Between 1880 and 1884 Cologne cathedral was the tallest building in the world and today is Germany's most popular tourist attraction receiving on average over 20,000 visitors per day! A perfect choice for my next cathedral climb!

During World War II the cathedral was hit 14 times by aerial bombs but did not collapse, it remained standing in an otherwise flattened city! Some people thought it was divine intervention but the more likely explanation is that the spires were a point of reference for the pilots!

There are 533 steps up to the viewing platform of 97.25 metres. Dad, yet again, was deposited for the third time in the pews along with our bags while we set off to the south tower for our climb. I totally forgot to record how long it took us to climb but I remember getting to St

Peter's bell and hoping that we were at the top but no such luck! St Peter's Bell is fascinating because it is the largest freely swinging bell in the world and weighs 24 tonnes!

The continuing spiral staircase was making Pete feel giddy so he was very grateful when we finally reached the top. We admired the view for a few minutes before making our way down again. So 97 metres away from 1484 means we only have 1387 metres to go! I think I've managed to make it sound like it's not many – that's a mistake – it's loads! This challenge might well end up being the hardest of them all! I could have put in photographs showing the view from the top of these cathedrals but as my challenge is climbing steps I felt it was more important to show me doing just that!

Cost: €3 each

10th May

We flew home today from Dusseldorf having enjoyed a relaxing week on board the 'Swiss Tiara' riverboat which easily qualified for another one of my mile challenges. The Swiss Tiara is a 5 star riverboat which carries 140 passengers and 35 crew members. It was built in 2006 and is 360 foot long. It is very luxurious and nothing is too much trouble for the crew who were exceptional. In my opinion a riverboat cruise is the perfect way to relax and unwind. I hope that doesn't mean I'm starting to get or sound old!

Travelling down the Rhine which is 1233 kilometres long (766 miles) we went through Switzerland, France and Germany. The river's source is in the Swiss Alps and it empties into the North Sea in the Netherlands. It is Germany's biggest river and is used by many river boat companies to ferry people up and down stopping at such interesting places such as Koblenz, Speyer and Bonn. It was also interesting to go through the huge locks and see all the big working barges.

Of course the real challenge of the week was trying to get through all the food! A huge cooked breakfast was followed by a four course lunch and usually a five course dinner. All of this with doing no exercise whatsoever to balance things up, apart from the climbing challenges I mentioned earlier. I'm dreading getting on the scales when I get home!

Cost: zero!

11th May

Oh my god!! I got on the scales this morning and was shocked to discover that I have gained 4.2 pounds in one week! I know everyone gains weight on holiday but our river cruise with course after course being laid down in front of us three times a day has done untold damage My weight is 11 stone 12 pounds (only 2.08 pounds lighter than when I started back in January!) and my fat is at 40.5 %!!! That's horrendous but not a complete surprise after all the food I've been knocking back. Why is it that fat is so easy to go on and yet so hard to get off? Serious action is needed. Fortunately I've still got loads of time before my party so I've no need to panic yet, but I must rein myself in tightly now, go to lots of boot camp sessions and cut back hard on my eating. I still have 6 months to go, so I must just put this behind me now and focus, focus, focus!!!! Dad stayed the night with us as we were due to go on a helicopter flight today. Point of note – Dad refused to get on the scales as he thought the shock may be too much for him at his age!

Felix had been on his own for the last week and had missed going to boot camp so we vowed to go at least two or three times this coming week. Hopefully that will help with my weight. Back to today and my 30th challenge is a helicopter ride for five minutes with my dad from our local airport – Blackbushe. For £28 each we got five minutes flight during which we flew for six miles. I paid a little extra to get a front seat for Dad as he had never been in a helicopter before.

The company that I booked the flight with was 'Adventure 001'. We were told to bring two forms of identification (neither of which were asked for!). Our scheduled flight time was 10:30am but we didn't actually take off until after 1pm! First the pilot had to go and refuel, okay I'm happy with that, but then we had to hang around for about one and a half hours while he decided whether the weather conditions were safe! Personally I think he went off to have lunch and blow the customers, they can wait! Poor Dad was freezing as it was so windy and exposed up there on the airfield. He waited in the car with Pete and I waited by the take-off point relaying news back to them regarding the delay. There were loads of other disgruntled customers there as well, and we were all moaning about the delays and our mood was not helped by the wind which seemed to get right through to our bones! One man there only had a long sleeved t-shirt on and he was actually starting to look blue around his mouth! We nearly gave up and went home but eventually the pilot decided it was okay so Dad and I got our flight. Dad was in the front next to the pilot and I was squashed in the back with two others. At least I did have a window seat so I could look out.

In the information they gave us the experience was described as 'helicopter buzz (six mile) pleasure flight'. I don't know if buzz was the type of helicopter they used or whether the name was referring to the sound it made as it buzzed about. The flight was enjoyable as we flew over the local area but at only five minutes long it was over all too soon.

Was the five minutes flight worth the two and a half hour wait? Absolutely not! Had it just been a helicopter flight we wouldn't have waited, but as it eliminated another of my challenges we had no choice but to wait. Also for Dad to have a new experience at 88 years old is great, and he did really enjoy it. I am halfway through these challenges now and ahead of schedule!

Cost: £59.00 (Dad and me)

16th May

Today Pete and I were off to Dartmouth Music Festival for the weekend. This year there were eight of us going – Geoff and Vanessa, Bru and Jenny, Steve and Dave (not a couple, just two single male friends whose wives are unable to come!) We all planned to meet at Buckfastleigh for lunch at 1pm as we were all coming from different directions. Pete and I thought that this would be a good opportunity to leave home early and go to Exeter Cathedral en-route to see if we could add another climb to my cathedral challenge.

We got there in good time having allowed one and a half hours to climb the cathedral as many times as we could in the time we had. Well, as often happens plans don't always work, and when we got there the lady on the desk said that the tower can only be climbed when on a tour of the cathedral, and there were no tours today! I asked if we could climb it on our own but she absolutely refused. Health and safety would not allow it! So we left and wandered around Exeter, had a coffee and cake and carried on with our journey to meet up with our friends.

This cathedral challenge is going to be more difficult than I thought – I might have to rethink!

17th May

Dartmouth is a wonderful town set on the western bank of the estuary of the River Dart. Opposite on the other bank is the town of Kingswear. There are two ferries which shuttle between the two towns – the 'lower ferry' is one, which operates from slips directly in the centre of both towns. Although it is more convenient, the traffic does have to negotiate the narrow streets of Kingswear which is no mean feat! It is owned and operated by South Hams District Council. This ferry can carry eight cars and is operated by unpowered ferry pontoons which are pushed and pulled by a tug boat.

The 'higher ferry' is a conventional vehicular cable ferry using the cables for propulsion as well as for guidance. It is also provided with four thrusters, one positioned at each corner, in order to provide additional manoeuvrability when operating in strong winds and tidal conditions. This ferry crosses the river Dart to the north to allow the A379 road between Kingsbridge and Torbay to bypass the narrow streets in the centre of Kingswear and Dartmouth. It is owned and operated by Dartmouth-Kingswear Floating Bridge Company and a toll is charged. The 'higher ferry' can carry 36 cars and came into service in late June 2009 and is officially known as 'The Floating Bridge' and of course being Dartmouth where there is no shortage of pubs, there is a pub nearby called 'The Floating Bridge'. There is no timetable as it just goes back and forth continually.

I decided that this would be a slightly different challenge from the norm so I was very happy to do it. In fact I was delighted when the man approached me to ask for my fare and decided not to charge me after I explained what I was doing, and why I wouldn't be getting off straightaway. Well he was absolutely lovely and didn't charge me a penny! I asked him the distance we would be travelling on each crossing. He said the distance was 416 metres, and he explained to me that 416 metres was the chain length, so I worked out I would have to do six crossings totalling 2760 metres because some of the chain was on the land and that would have to be deducted. Each trip was 50p so I saved £3! I started at 2:33pm and the challenge was completed at 3:03pm. Each journey was three minutes and the rest of the time was taken up with loading and unloading the cars.

My friends were all in The Floating Bridge pub sat outside in the sunshine. When the challenge was over I thanked the man very much and went to the top of the chain to measure the distance between where it was fastened to the quay and the water's edge. I paced it out to be 40 paces but being only 5 foot 2 inches and having to do big strides my friends fell about laughing as I think I reminded them of John Cleese and the 'Ministry of Silly Walks'! It's funny how when you get older you don't worry so much about making a fool of yourself!

Anyway, assuming it is 40 metres also on the Kingswear side of the river that equals 80m x 6 = 480 metres to be deducted. So 2760-480 equals 2280 metres. I only needed to do 1610 metres! Oh well never mind so much for my maths abilities, but better too much than not enough!

Cost: zero!

18th May

A beautiful sunny day greeted us when we woke. Steve, Jenny and I decided to have a river cruise on the 'Kingswear Castle'. This is the last remaining coal-fired paddle steamer in operation in the UK today and uses half a ton of coal daily. She was built in 1924 by Philip and Son of Dartmouth. She was loaned to the US Navy during World War II for use as a harbour tender. Later she was bought by the 'Paddle Steamer Preservation Society' and was moved to Chatham in Kent where they spent 15 years restoring her to her former glory, so she looked her best while offering river trips on the Medway since 1985. In 2012 she returned to the home waters of the River Dart after an absence of 47 years!

The commentator on board was a chap called Reggie and he was brilliant at injecting lots of humour to his anecdotes which really added to the joy of the afternoon. He even offered to take us all to the Caribbean although that may have been in jest! He was so passionate about the boat and it showed, which is really quite a skill when you have to repeat the same commentary over and over!

The trip lasted one and a quarter hours and we travelled two miles up the river to Dittisham where there is a pedestrian ferry to Greenway Quay. This is adjacent to the Greenway Estate which is now owned by the National Trust and open to the public as it is the former home of the late Agatha Christie. Dittisham is also famous for the Dittisham

plum which is grown there. At Dittisham we turned around and went down the river and eventually out to sea. We were all excited for a while with thoughts of the Caribbean but sadly it was not to be! In all we covered a distance of about four miles.

Steve took this photo of me and I asked him to try and get the paddle in the photo. He was hanging off the side as best he could, but he failed in securing the photo of the paddle. Short of jumping into the sea it was never going to work!

I did wonder why a boat is always referred to as 'she' and the following was written by a George Moses in Falmouth, Massachusetts which in my view sums it up very well: *"A boat is called a she because there's always a great deal of bustle around her... because there's usually a gang of men around... because she has waist and stays... because she takes a lot of paint to keep her looking good... because it's not the initial expense that breaks you, it's the upkeep... because she is all decked out... because it takes a good man to handle her right... because she shows her topside, hides her bottom and, when coming into port, always heads for the buoys."*

I would strongly recommend this trip if ever you find yourselves in that part of the world because it was great and a perfect way to while away a sunny afternoon.

Cost: £15

21st May

Today is Wednesday and after work today Pete, Felix and I drove up to North Wales so we were ready for our trip to Zip World tomorrow at our allotted time of 10.30am. Zip World is over Penrhyn Quarry at Bethesda and has the longest zip wire in Europe. There are two specially constructed and spectacular zip wires there, which give participants the thrill of a lifetime! The nearest thing to actually flying that you'll ever experience! After a long four and a half hour drive which Pete and I shared, we eventually arrived at Abbeyfield Hotel in Bangor at about 7.50pm. We didn't stop on the journey as Pete had bought provisions during the day which we just ate while travelling. I think when you have a long drive you just want to get there and with two drivers it's no problem. The hotel was well positioned for tomorrow with it only being a five or ten minute drive away to get to the zip wire.

Abbeyfield Hotel was really a pub with rooms, quite old fashioned looking but clean, and I would like to say comfortable but the truth is the mattresses were extremely firm and gave me backache. Pete, to save money, had booked us all into a triple room and unfortunately none of us enjoyed a good night's sleep. Pete couldn't get comfortable, I had backache and kept getting pins and needles in my hand and arm and Felix complained that both Pete and I snored! According to him we snored all night long and at one point he recorded us on his phone. He has played it back to us and I have to say it must be Pete as I am far too much of a lady to make grunting noises like that! At 4.30am when, as Felix puts it, 'he had had no sleep whatsoever, none, nil, zilch, zero' he decided to text his three brothers to share with them his distress at not being able to sleep. Unsurprisingly he didn't receive any replies at that time but I guess it made him feel better reaching out for some sympathy.

22nd May

The new day dawned with Felix in a really foul mood. Pete and I tried not to talk to him unless we absolutely had to. Felix told us that he was texting his friends at 4am looking for sympathy to his plight of still being awake – I can only guess at how popular he was with his friends at *that* moment!

The three of us made it to breakfast where we all tucked into eggs, bacon, sausage, mushrooms, beans, tomatoes and toast. It was excellent! It also had the added benefit of improving Felix's mood although as we had an hour to kill before we needed to leave he did retreat back to bed!

We arrived at Zip World by 10.30am and got kitted up in red boiler suits, helmets and goggles. There were nine of us in our group, and for the £50 each that we have paid we would get a ride on the 'Little Zipper' (which is a taster of what was to come) where you reach speeds of about 40mph. This would be followed by a quarry tour ride, then the best bit, which was the ride on the 'Big Zipper'.

After a safety briefing we set off for a walk of about 400 metres to the start of the 'Little Zipper'. There are two zip lines so that means that two people can go down at the same time side by side. Felix and I decided to go down together and Pete would follow in the next run. I was babbling a lot which is a sure sign that I was a bit nervous! The staff members were lovely and very reassuring, so I soon felt better and allowed myself to feel excited. Felix and I were strapped in horizontally and then the staff shouted, '3, 2, 1 go!'

Wow it was amazing! I loved it but it was over far too quickly! I immediately wanted to do it again! The length of this small zipper is

500 metres (1650 feet) with a maximum speed of 40mph. The maximum height above the ground on this zipper is 22 metres (72 feet). When it was Pete's turn he really flew, and for a moment he thought he wasn't going to stop at the other end but the staff reached out and grabbed his hand which slowed him down.

We were all on a high from this when this red converted army truck pulled up and we all bundled inside ready for our quarry tour. Well, it wouldn't start! The engine sounded so close to starting but just wouldn't quite catch. Anyway, after about 10 minutes a replacement truck pulled up so we abandoned the truck we were in and clambered aboard the second one.

We went up and up along this windy track until we reached a height of 152 metres. The onboard commentary was excellent. We learnt little snippets about the quarry, for example it was once the largest slate quarry in the world and infamously it is where the longest strike in British industrial history took place.

When we got off the views were magnificent over the blue water of the slate quarry with Snowdonia's mountains in the background – really a sight to behold! On this zip wire ride it was decided that this time Felix would go down first with some other guy so that he could take a photo of Pete and me coming in doing our 'superman impressions'. (Had to be done I'm afraid!) In no time at all it was our turn and facing downwards horizontally from so high up really was quite something! Surprisingly I didn't feel at all nervous and was far more excited this time round. The '3, 2, 1 go' rang out and we were off! It was totally awesome!

The 'flight' for want of a better word lasted about 60 seconds and as before, as soon as I got off I wanted to do it again! We all agreed it was brilliant fun. We walked back down to the reception to remove our kit and go the photo booth to see how our photo turned out which was taken as we came down. Here is mine:

Of course you can't judge how fast I was going but the maximum speed possible on the 'Big Zipper' is 115mph (185kmh). I was nowhere near that fast as I was not completely horizontal, but it was certainly fast enough for me! The length of the 'Big Zipper' is 1560 metres which is a little short of the mile but as I did the 'Little Zipper' first so job done!

We had a really good time and it improved Felix's mood enormously, but with a four and a half hour drive and a cost of £150 plus £80 for the hotel it won't be happening again soon! The best challenge so far though!

Cost: £50 each plus £80 for the hotel.

We left Bangor at approximately 1pm and as our route took us past Chester, Pete and I decided to call in at Chester Cathedral to take the opportunity to climb the tower (if it had one that is.)

We left Felix in the car, as he wanted to sleep, and went in search of the cathedral.

It was open so that was a promising start but that was as promising as it got because unless we were with a tour we were not allowed to climb the tower! I asked quite earnestly if we could please climb it on our own but my request was declined – health and safety you know!

Oh dear, that's the second cathedral we've been forbidden from climbing on our own. They don't seem to be so fussy abroad, it's just in the UK that I'm having problems. Not giving up just yet though…

26th May

Why, oh why after gaining so much weight on my river cruise and more importantly vowing to knock it straight off, why then is my weight today 11 stone 12.2 pounds? My fat is still 40.5 %! Of course, I have been to Dartmouth Music Festival with our friends since the river cruise, where we have a cooked breakfast every morning and eat out every night of which one night is always fish and chips and another is invariably a curry! Then of course there's lunch which is often a Cornish pasty and in the afternoon if the weather is sunny, an ice cream is tempting, oh and there is a lovely café in Dartmouth that just does the best Devonshire cream teas! I think I have spotted the problem!

Still, there is still plenty of time until November I must not get despondent as that will not help my resolve. Put it behind me and move on…

I am vote counting tonight so I hope they don't lay on any food although I suspect there will be nibbles or sweets or something, hope I'm strong enough to resist or maybe it's best to think that today is ruined anyway and start again tomorrow!

29th May

It was not a very bright day today but at least it wasn't raining. Felix and I went to boot camp in the morning and although I'd got a lot to do at home, for example weed the whole garden, I suggested to Pete that we should go to Hollycombe Steam in the Country Museum at Liphook. It is a museum of national importance and you can experience the atmosphere and power of steam in all its glory spanning its many applications from the early 19th century onwards. The collection at Hollycombe includes items from the traditional fairground, steam railways and road engines to the farm and estate machinery. My mission today was to travel a mile on a carousel (steam powered of course!)

There were not a lot of people there today, probably due to the unsettled weather and the staff members seemed a bit thin on the ground. I asked Pete to calculate how many revolutions I needed to do. He starts by asking an employee the diameter of the roundabout and is told 42 or 44 foot edge to edge. Pete assumes the lowest of 42 foot. The distance of the edge of the carousel to the horse is 3 foot (measured). The diameter of the circle travelled by the horse per revolution is 36x3.142 = 113 feet (say 100 for luck!) One mile equals 1760 yards, so 1760x3 = 5280 feet. The number of revolutions required is 5280÷100 = 52.8 required for the mile so let's say 53.

Pete had to do it as accurately as he could for his own satisfaction, and because I asked him to. I didn't want there to be any chance of me

not completing the full mile. I feel the least I could do is to demonstrate how he reached the conclusions that he did.

I told the employee Jason what I was doing and he loved the idea but said that I wouldn't get 53 revolutions out of one turn. I told him that was fine; I would just ride the carousel as many times as I needed to. Jason was in charge of two fairground rides, so after my first time I had to wait around while he had to see to the other ride. In all I had to have three sessions on the carousel and the third session was really long as he struggled to keep the music going while the revolutions clocked up. In all I completed 55 laps which easily covered the mile – well done Jason! This challenge took me 52 minutes.

This photograph is of a boiler that used to be in a wood mill to drive saw equipment. It is now used at Hollycombe to produce steam which is piped off to work three of the fairground rides. After I finished my challenge Pete and I then had a bit of lunch in the café, followed by a ride on the steam train but I wasn't counting that for my train challenge as I had got other ideas for that!

Cost: £14 for me and £12 for Pete

31st May

Having completed 34 challenges I am well ahead of schedule. I know I have to do five per month so it would be okay if I had only done 25 but I've done 34 – yippee!

As the weather was a little overcast today Pete and I trekked over to Salisbury which took about one hour. The plan was to climb the cathedral steps. I decided to check online before we left to see what time the tower opened, only to find out that we could only go up the tower if we were booked onto a tour! We were too late to book online so we phoned them and managed to book onto the 11:15am tour. We paid over the phone and with no concessions for Pete who is 65, it cost us £10 each for the tour which lasts for one hour and 45 minutes. We got there just in time but I missed the first few minutes of the tour as I had to go and search for a loo having drunk a large mug of tea just before leaving home.

Ian Henderson, our guide, was very good and with 12 in our party we were all able to hear what was being said. Salisbury Cathedral has Britain's tallest spire at 123m (404 foot.) It has stunning early English Gothic architecture and the oldest working mechanical clock in the world dating from about AD 1386 (supposedly!) The foundation stone of the cathedral was laid in 1220, and the main body of the cathedral was completed in just 38 years by 1258. The spire was added a little later. It was very interesting going up into the roof of the cathedral and seeing all the medieval wooden scaffolding. Christopher Wren was called in 1660 to add diagonal ties across the tower because the tower walls began to move outwards due to the estimated 300 tons of horizontal thrust from relieving squinch arches in the top of the tower. Our tour to the top of the tower was a climb of 332 steps, most of it up the spiral stone staircase but some of it in contraptions such as in this photo.

It's a good job I'm not fatter than I am as I might've struggled! The highest we were allowed to go was 68 metres above the ground. You can see from this photo that the staircase is very narrow and having a tour to the top really is the only way, because at least all the traffic is either going up or coming down. Passing on the staircase would have been scary to say the least!

This photograph was taken looking to the west over the water.

A question for you – our lovely guide, who must've been about 70, stressed to all of us that the climb would be quite challenging and only to start if we were sure we could finish, so why, oh why did we get to the first level only for one couple to say they couldn't go on? Poor Ian had to radio down to get another staff member to come up and escort them down, and meanwhile the rest of us all had to wait! I think I may be turning into a grumpy old woman!

Total 1387-68 = 1319m to go!

Cost: £10 each

This evening I spent a few minutes on my laptop looking for place to waterski. Unfortunately they don't do it at Horseshoe Lake where I did my other water challenges, so I'm looking further afield. I thought I would try and combine it with a visit to Moors Valley Country Park near Ringwood where I know they have Segway rides. In my search I come across CJM Ski and Wake at Ellingham who do waterskiing on the lakes at Blashford. I email them and tell them about my challenge and the fact I'm a complete novice, and within a few hours I get a reply from Chris Mullins who would be delighted to help me! Cutting to the chase I am now booked in for this Thursday at 10am.

JUNE

4th June

From work I phone Moors Valley to enquire about their Segway rides for tomorrow. Waterskiing is booked for 10am. I guess training, health and safety chat plus getting changed will take a couple of hours, so I am looking to book two segways at 1 o'clock-ish. Unfortunately the only times they have available are 3:40pm or 5 o'clock. It looks like we'll have to have a long leisurely lunch somewhere first!

5th June

It is 9:40am and Pete and I have arrived at CJM Ski and Wake Board Coaching which is at Ellingham Waterski and Wakeboard Club near Ringwood. We are met by Chris Mullins - obviously the 'CJM' who makes us very welcome.

When I emailed Chris the other day, he replied that first of all I would hold onto the bar on the side of the boat, and then he would get me to hold onto the rope behind the boat as you're supposed to do. I thought okay maybe, when I got his email but now I was there I didn't feel nearly so confident! The weather was lovely and Pete and I were the only ones there. I was given a wetsuit and disappeared to the changing room ready for my ordeal (sorry I mean challenge!) I emerged after a few minutes suitably attired in wetsuit and lifejacket and with hair tied back. Pete was going to ride on the boat with Chris and hopefully take some good photos. On the pontoon Chris gave me some instructions about how to stand when we got going as in keep my arms straight and push up through my legs. I practised on the pontoon and felt quietly confident that I could do this. Chris helped me to put on my skis and I gingerly entered the lake from the back of the boat. It was freezing but the water soon warmed up next to my skin. I inched my way round to the pole on the side of the boat and hung on for dear life! Chris told me to put my heels to my bum, arms straight and then stand up when he tells me. Okay, I was ready, I was off! Unfortunately I didn't go anywhere! I lurched forwards and went headlong into the lake and my skis fell off! Putting them back on is unbelievably difficult. I had to hold onto the boat, put my foot in the air so I could put the ski on and then reach down to pull the tab at the back of my heel. Chris helped me but I found it really tiring – absolutely exhausting work!

This photograph was my second attempt to stand up, and just look at the concentration on my face! My arms are straight, and I did do a little better than my first attempt. It is so much harder than it looks, and requires a lot of physical effort. Again my skis came off, so I had to go through the whole nightmare of getting them back on again – I'm not sure if this wasn't the hardest bit of the whole challenge.

This photo shows my third attempt, and please notice that I am upright! Chris was shouting at me from the boat, 'Don't move!' while he clocked up the distance for me.

After the mile was completed I dropped into the lake so pleased that I managed it. This was the first challenge I'd done where I seriously doubted I could do it, and possibly the hardest so far. It took 25 minutes which was good of Chris as I only paid him £24 for 15 minutes. He must have had loads more confidence in me than I had if he really thought I could do it all in 15 minutes. As for the rope from the back of the boat – it never happened! Before we left I asked Chris how fast the boat was going. I was thinking 50mph only to be told 15mph – oh my goodness I can't believe it as it felt so much faster than that!

Here is a smiley photograph to illustrate the relief of a successful challenge, as I climbed back onto the boat.

Cost: £24

We left Ellingham Waterski and Wakeboard Club at about 11am. I phoned my dad to see if we could go and visit him for few hours, before having to return to Ringwood in time for the Segway tour at Moors Valley. Unfortunately he wasn't in, which, as it turned out, worked out quite well as I then phoned Moors Valley to recheck the timings of the Segway tours that day, and was told that the next tour was 11.40am! Absolutely perfect – how often do things work out as well as that? We arrived there about 11.20am so even had time for a coffee first which I desperately needed after all of my efforts on the waterskis! Not absolutely sure I needed the flapjack coated with thick caramel to accompany the coffee, but I felt I deserved it. The cost to hire the Segway was £35 each, which I thought was a bit steep but it had to be done. James the instructor was lovely, and the only other person riding with us was George who was a staff member in training. We were issued with helmets and had about a 10 minute training and practice session before being allowed off into the woods.

It was a lovely day and we covered approximately 3 miles through virtually deserted forest. It was good but sort of boring. We have been lucky enough to have done it before in Rome, which was much better as there was a lot to look at, and you also had the sport of trying not to knock down pedestrians! Here there are only trees, and they don't tend to jump out at you!

When we had finished we had a look at the 'Go Ape' course which they have there. I believe the course is about 1000 metres long, which is less than the mile, but perhaps I could do it one and a bit times, or maybe twice on two separate occasions, as these 'Go Ape' treetop adventures are all over the country. It looks hard but one of the challenges on my list is abseiling which I have decided to rule out, so I do need a replacement. This may just fit the bill – challenging but doable, whereas abseiling is just ridiculous. What was I thinking?!

The entrance into Moors Valley Country Park was £7.80 so we paid our bill and left. I phoned Dad again and he was still out, so we went into Ringwood and had lunch in a lovely cafe where it was warm enough to sit outside. I had a look in some shops for a party dress for my 60th birthday for this coming November, but I didn't see anything I liked. I rang Dad again – hallelujah he was in! We drove over to visit him but didn't feel we could turn up empty-handed so we bought him an Eccles cake (which I know to be a favourite of his!) Pete chose a Chelsea bun and I chose a lemon doughnut to have with our afternoon cup of tea. It's no wonder I'm not losing weight!

Cost: £35 each plus £7.80

7th June

Freddie is home for the weekend with a surprise for us! It's our 35th wedding anniversary this weekend and we are taking all of the family to Tylney Hall Hotel for afternoon tea. His surprise, or rather shock for us, was that he has had a tattoo done! Not one, but two! Around his ankle he has the family portrayed as stick men all holding hands, and on his forearm he now has an oak leaf to symbolise his wish to get back to nature – I'm not happy! It doesn't look too bad now, but it will look so ridiculous when he's 60 or so! Freddie is so thrilled with them however, so I try hard not to moan too much as I have no wish to deflate him, but I think he gets it that I'm not too keen. Pete is also disappointed, but like he says, it's his body and his life. What can you do – kids eh!

8th June

My weight today is 11 stone 9.6 pounds with my fat content still sitting at 40.5%. On a positive note I am 2.6 pounds down on the last fortnight so that's good. That averages out at just over 1 pound per week which I need to lose, which is ideal and hopefully I should be able to maintain that. Tomorrow is our 35th wedding anniversary and at least if I indulge, which really is a given, I do at least have 13 days before I need to report again! Hopefully I should be able to continue with a weight loss – fingers crossed anyway! This afternoon we all went for afternoon tea at a local hotel to celebrate our anniversary and no, I didn't think about my weight or skimp on my food!

9th June

Today is our 35th wedding anniversary – coral I think. Unfortunately I have to go to work first until 3pm before we set off for London. Pete decided that we'd drive up, and as we got in the car I noticed that the refuel light was on. I mentioned that it might be a good idea to fill up now as there aren't many garages in central London, but Pete is on a mission and wants to get going. The journey to London is only 45 miles but as we pull into the underground car park near to the Strand Palace Hotel where we're staying, I noticed that the car displays only five miles worth of fuel left! Pete was playing it cool, and if he was worried he's certainly wasn't sharing it with me!

We checked into the hotel and went up to the room to dump our bags. We had booked tickets to see 'Fatal Attraction' at the Theatre Royal in Haymarket. I remembered seeing the film many years ago and loved it – a bit of a warning to all men who may be tempted to stray! The show started at 7.30pm so we walked to the theatre, and then once we knew where we were we looked for somewhere to eat.

Directly opposite we saw 'Spaghetti House' and Pete and I chose a table, looked at the menu, then ordered a spaghetti carbonara for two people. After a few minutes it was served in this lovely earthenware crock with a lid to keep the heat in, and I have to say that it was absolutely delicious! We devoured it like we'd never seen food before!

It was warm enough to sit outside just 'people watching' – a particularly interesting pastime in London where there is such diversity. We passed on the option of a dessert as there was an ice cream tub in the theatre with our name on it! We both agreed the spaghetti carbonara was the best we had ever had. It was seriously good!

I've decided that Pete is a very naughty man, and possibly the cause of my inability to lose weight! We no sooner entered the theatre when he said, 'Do you want some sweets?' He knows I'm weak so of course I said yes, expecting him to buy a bag of Minstrels for us to share, but no – a whole bag of Maltesers for me and a bag of Minstrels for him! At least mine had less fattening centres! I'm ashamed to say that by the interval both bags were finished! One strawberry tub later and my body was telling me that I had seriously overindulged. My stomach was very distended and I felt a bit sick, but couldn't blame anybody as it was nobody's fault but mine.

Why don't I stop when I've had enough rather than keep on eating until I can squeeze no more in? It must be something to do with celebrating as eating and drinking always feature highly as a social pastime to share with friends. Who am I kidding? I can eat this much when just at home as the truth is I enjoy eating and love food! There, I've said it. Now, rather like an alcoholic admitting he's an alcoholic is the first step to getting help, why isn't there a similar thing for food lovers to go to so they can get help? Thinking about it I guess there is Weight Watchers and Slimming World plus others I'm sure.

Anyway, moving on, Pete and I loved the play and we both agreed it was much better than we thought it was going to be.

That evening in the hotel we exchanged anniversary cards. I gave him a voucher to go on the Orient Express as my 'train' challenge. He had always wanted to go so he was thrilled! I hoped he noticed it was just a day trip to Canterbury and not Venice!

10th June

We are spending the day in London to knock off a couple more challenges. After a hearty cooked breakfast we were well fuelled for what was ahead. We started by walking to St Paul's Cathedral where we hoped to do more of my 'step' challenge.

The cost to go in was £16.50 for me and £14.50 for Pete which I thought was rather expensive, so to get our money's worth we decided to climb to the Golden Gallery twice.

The first climb took about an hour as on each gallery we stopped to take photos and didn't rush ourselves at all. In fact I had a lovely chat with one of the staff at the top and told her about my challenge – she loved the idea and wished me the very best of luck with it! The second climb Pete and I tried to do as quickly as possible – 10 minutes start to finish, not bad at all!

This photo is after my first climb as I still look like I have some energy left, which I assure you, was not the case after the second assent! Coming back down was not a problem as there were different steps for the most part anyway. We visited the cafe as I was desperate for water as I felt dehydrated after an upset stomach the previous night, the details of which I will spare you. Let's just say overindulgence is not good for the body, but will I ever learn?

There are 528 steps up to the Golden Gallery, which is a height of 85 metres. We climbed it twice so that is 85m x 2 = 170m. Taking this total off the remainder left after our Salisbury Cathedral climb, leaves 1149m to go! Before we leave we go down to the crypt. Pete worked out that the steps measured 175mm x 37 (number of steps) = 6475mm divided by 1000 = 6.475m. Let's call it six metres. Total now 1149 - 6 = 1143m (so much better!)

Pete and I have decided that this 'step' challenge cannot be completed by climbing cathedrals alone, so any steps will do, but I can't just count the steps at home, they must be in notable buildings!

Cost: £16.50 + £14.50 (Total £31)

While we are in London we are determined to have a ride in a rickshaw, as it's a lot cheaper than flying out to China, and to be honest I don't know where else we would find one! There didn't seem to be any rickshaws around St Paul's, so Pete suggested we get the tube train to Covent Garden where he thought there were bound to be plenty as it's a popular tourist destination. It was a good idea, and of course the tube train counts as another one of my 60! The underground station at St Paul's was not leaping out at us. Pete was forced to ask a fellow pedestrian, which, as we all know, would have made him feel very uncomfortable. Men find it extremely difficult, because somehow their brains are wired that asking directions is a complete no-no! Anyway, that hurdle overcome, we travelled on the Central line to Holborn and then changed to the Piccadilly line and to Covent Garden.

It's funny but you have no idea of the distance you're travelling on the tube, and when I got home, I Googled it just to ensure I had travelled the mile. St Paul's to Holborn took six minutes and was a distance of 0.97 miles and Holborn to Covent Garden took four minutes and was less than half a mile. Phew just done it!

Cost: £4.70 each

Arriving at Covent Garden by tube necessitates going into a lift to reach ground level. It is one of the deepest stations but not *the* deepest as that prize goes to Hampstead at 192 feet below ground level. I asked Pete if we could find somebody we could ask permission from to climb the steps instead. Fortunately the man we found was very obliging, although I think he did wonder why we would want to. Pete explained that we were 'into' steps so goodness knows what he made of that!

Pete calculated the riser of the steps measured seven inches and there were 193 of them so 193 x 7 = 1351 inches which converts to 34.31 metres. Let's call it 34 metres. The running total is now 1143-34 = 1109.

Covent Garden was bathed in the most glorious sunshine; it really was a beautiful day. As soon as we emerged from the tube station we saw in front of us lots of rickshaws and cyclists waiting for a fare – how lucky is that? We looked along the row and chose a young man whose name I found out was Pavel from Poland. I guess most people say where they want to go, but we just said, 'Can you take us anywhere as long as you cover a mile in distance?' Not a request he had obviously had before, so again we had to explain about my challenge and although his English was good, I'm sure I provided him with the proof that the expression 'Mad English' was in fact true! Still, I'm not worried about that as I think these challenges are fun! Pavel said the fare would be £5 and Pete took this photo just before we set off.

We went down the Strand and Whitehall, over Westminster Bridge, along the Southbank to Waterloo, across Waterloo Bridge, and back to the Strand. I completely forgot to time the journey, but I know Pavel was saying that he didn't understand why there was so much traffic today, so I guess our ride was taking him longer than he expected. I found it absolutely amazing how he wove in between the traffic, almost dangerously at times. I feel to drive in London safely you could really do with a head which can swivel 360 degrees! Pete and I jumped out at some traffic lights in the Strand and gave Pavel an extra £10 to help him. It's the first time I know of where we've given a tip which amounts to more than the cost, but he was a nice guy and we're no lightweights! When we got home we worked out the distance Pavel took us and it was about 2.4 miles.

Cost: £15

As the day ended, it was time to go home. I thought 'this is going to be interesting'. The car did start, and Pete thought (wisely) we should try and get some petrol, as the 5 registered miles left was *not* going to get us home! On his sat nav he typed in garages and we followed the directions, only to give up fairly rapidly as the traffic was at a standstill. We certainly didn't have the fuel for the car to be idling. Pete returned to his sat nav and looked for the next garage listed and we made for that. When we got there the garage was boarded up and had been for some time! Back to the sat nav again and the third garage listed nearby was our next destination. By now the car was running on vapours and stress levels were rising! Now I don't know if guardian angels are real or not, but we managed to buy petrol at Pete's third attempt, thank goodness. His stress levels subsided but mine hung around for a bit as I felt it was all so unnecessary. If only he had listened to me before we had left home and filled up the car like I suggested!

12th June

A while ago Pete phoned the Spinnaker Tower in Portsmouth to see if he could arrange for us to visit and climb the steps to the top. The reply came back 'yes' as long as a staff member came with us.

Well today is the day. We were delighted to meet up with Adam, who was the duty manager assigned the task of taking us to the top. The Spinnaker Tower is the centrepiece of the redevelopment of Portsmouth Harbour. It was supported by a National Lottery grant. Its shape is modelled after a sail to reflect Portsmouth's maritime history. The tower was opened on 18th October 2005, and impressively stands at a height of 170 metres. This makes it two and a half times taller than Nelson's Column. To ascend by lift takes less than 30 seconds to a height of 110 metres. This takes you to the viewing platform and the highest we can go. We however, were climbing the 570 steps – no luxury of a lift for us! Surprisingly, we didn't find it too tiring although I did need to stop a couple of times for a quick breather. It only took us 10 minutes to reach the top and I was dead keen to do it again. Unfortunately though, Adam had a meeting so couldn't allow us to do it again as we were not allowed to climb it unescorted. My personal feeling is that he was too tired and made the whole 'meeting' thing up!

We thanked him very much and spent a few minutes on the viewing platform absorbing the fantastic views which stretch for 23 miles. I was even brave enough to walk over the glass floor which is not a comfortable experience, as you wonder if your weight is the one that will make the glass crack and you'll plummet to your death! Being a bit dramatic here! Adam was very kind as he only charged us £5 each even though normal adult admission is £8.95.

The Spinnaker Tower is an excellent attraction and has recently been named 'attraction of the year'. Note to self – I must bring the boys here as I think they'd really enjoy it, although perhaps not Marcus, as he's a bit scared of heights! Though I must stop thinking of them as boys as they're men! The running total now for the steps challenge is 1109 - 110 = 999 (under the thousand – great!)

When we left the Spinnaker Tower we looked around for other tall buildings to possibly climb and saw this tower, so made a beeline for it.

Its address is number one Gunwharf Quays and is a residential block of exclusive apartments. We entered through a revolving door to be greeted by two men who worked for Berkeley Homes, who own the building. They were looking at some plans of the building. Pete and I asked if it would be possible for us to climb the steps to the top. I told them why we would want to do this and they replied, 'Go fill your boots!' Great response, and at zero cost Pete and I wanted to make the most of this opportunity. The men told us it would be possible to climb up 27 floors with a total step count of 486. The height of the building to the 27th floor according to the man with the plan is 110.43 metres (let's say 110m).

The first climb up took us 10 minutes, and although we were chatting, we didn't find it too stressful or hard. Fortunately it wasn't a spiral, just lots and lots of staircases. We got the lift down and I decided to do it again. Of course the second time was not quite so easy, but still only took us 10 minutes. Pete surprises me at how well he does, he never seems puffed. I think he just takes it slowly, gets a steady pace going and keeps putting one foot in front of the other. I, on the other hand, start trying to show off by jumping up two at a time, then tire myself out and have to stop for a couple of minutes –

honestly I'm such a child! This illustrates our relationship really – father, daughter. He is all steady and reliable and I'm all skittish around him. Still, it seems to work okay, and everybody's relationship is different after all.

After the second time I suggested maybe doing the climb for a third time as this was such a good opportunity. I half hoped he would say no, that he'd had enough, but he said that if I wanted to then he would do it with me. Very little talking took place on this climb, and our time slipped to 11 minutes! This photo is taken on the 27th floor after the third climb up.

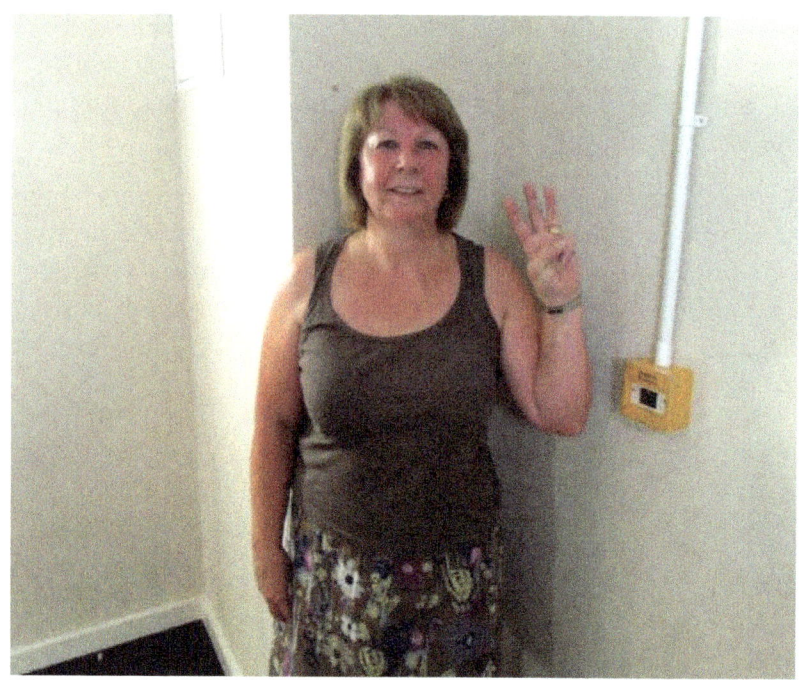

I'm very red-faced and the smile is forced, but I'm thrilled about the number of metres we've done in this one building. The shape of the building is meant to represent a funnel however locally it has been nicknamed 'lipstick towers!' The total number of metres left for the steps challenge is 999-(110x3) = 669.

14th June

Felix is celebrating his 25th birthday today! We are all going for a curry tonight in our favourite restaurant in a local village. It's a tradition that we've always done on someone's birthday and many times inbetween as well!

22nd June

My weight today is 11 stone 9.4 pounds with my fat being at the gross sum of 40%. Very, very slightly down on the weigh-in a fortnight ago but unfortunately it is nothing to get excited about! I think my age has a lot to do with it, as I am laying down fat to see me through my old age. I feel a bit depressed about it, but there is not a lot I can do about that, apart from keep on going to boot camp. At least that way I should at least be able to maintain my weight even if I struggle to lose it!

24th June

Nothing is planned for today apart from gardening, which seems endless at this time of year, but I'm conscious of the fact that I need to do another challenge. I haven't done one for two weeks now so I looked down my list to see what I could do that doesn't need planning or much effort. I decided upon the tram ride. I found out that although most trams seem to be in the north, for example Blackpool or Manchester, there is a tram link in Croydon. I asked Pete if he fancied a run out to Croydon, of course he didn't really – I mean who would? Pete is very kind natured though and realises that these challenges have to be done, and it is a lot closer than Blackpool! I have an aunt and uncle who live fairly near there, so I phoned them to see if they wanted to meet for lunch. They do, great! The journey to Croydon took us about one hour and we met up with Lin and Nev outside the Fairfield Halls Theatre. We took a short stroll to George Street where we bought our tram tickets to Wimbledon at a cost of £2.40 each. Lin and Nev didn't have to pay as they have free transport throughout all of London.

The tram link in Croydon began operating in May 2000 and carries 22 million passengers every year, which helps to ease the congestion on the roads. The line runs from New Addington to Wimbledon which is a distance of 28km with 39 stops. Our journey today from George

Street, Croydon to Wimbledon takes us 32 minutes and is well over 10km. Unfortunately Pete and I did not have a lot of time to browse around Wimbledon as we had to get home to meet Felix from work. We did, however, have time for a quick lunch and found quite a nice place in a shopping arcade. We all had paninis and very good they were too! When we had finished we strolled around a bit and came across this scene in the next photograph.

I thought it was funny to see people enjoying watching Wimbledon in Wimbledon! This is the first week and the weather is lovely and warm with not a hint of rain – how unusual for Wimbledon week!

I didn't quite catch it in the photograph but the yellow letters on the right say Murrison's instead of Morrison's – the well-known food chain! I just love that quirky British sense of humour!

Another 32 minutes and £2.40 each for the train back to George Street and it was time to say goodbye to Lin and Nev. We retrieved the car from the car park and drove home. I thought the car park was expensive at £10 but at least we didn't have to walk too far!

Cost: £10 plus £4.80 each

25th June

I phoned 'Go Ape' at Moors Valley in Ringwood to book Pete and I on to the treetop adventure for tomorrow at 10am. I don't feel very confident about this, and think that this may be the challenge I fail on. My personality is such that I'm so dogged and competitive that if Pete can do it I certainly won't give up without giving my all. Only time will tell!

Cost: £64

26th June

We arrived at Moors Valley 'Go Ape' about 20 minutes early so hung around for a bit. The staff suggested we go and get a coffee as they were not quite ready for us. Pete had one but not for me as I didn't want to be in the position of needing the loo after I was all harnessed up!

On our car journey down to Ringwood I rang Freddie, as he should have had his degree results. He had, and told us he achieved a 2:2 in Property Development and Planning. Of course we knew what the course was, but he obviously felt the need to remind us. I guess we should have been pleased, however Pete and I were really disappointed as all through this course he assured us he was on for a first or in the worst case a 2:1. We think he coasted in his last year and taken his eye off the ball. In particular his dissertation could have been better, although Freddie told us he was pleased with it. Oh well, nothing we can do about it now! The news though had definitely dampened our mood, and what with me being extremely anxious about what I was about to do, there was little conversation between us!

When I booked yesterday, Pete and I were the only ones who had booked for 10am. Some more people had obviously decided to make the most of the settled weather, because now there was a gathering of eight people all being introduced to Tom, our instructor. We got given

harnesses, which we all put on, and Tom came to each of us in turn to tighten the fastenings to make sure all is well. Next, we were given instructions as to how the carabiners operate – you can see here that I'm giving it my full attention. Also notice that I am old enough to be the mother of any of my fellow 'Go Apers', apart from Pete of course!

The course is divided into five sections; Tom stayed with us while we do sections one and two which are shorter in length. When he was happy we were then left on our own to make our way round the rest of the course. There are 39 obstacles over the 1000 metre course, and at the end of each section there is a zip wire, of which the longest is 166 metres at the end of section five. The chaps in the office worked out for me that to complete a mile I would have to do the five sections, that is the whole course, and then do sections three, four and five again. Okay, I'm up for this now.

To reach our first obstacle at the start of section three, we first had to climb a rope ladder – not that easy! We sensibly let the others in our group go ahead of us so that if Pete and I were a bit slower we wouldn't hold everybody else up. Sections one and two were quite short and Tom was there looking over us, but now we were on our own, and our life was in our hands so to speak. I conquered the rope ladder and stood on the platform securing myself with safety lines at all times. Carefully I made my way across the first crossing holding on tightly to the wire above my head, to which my safety lines and pulley were attached. Hurray I'd done it and my confidence started to soar! I could do this, and I started to really enjoy it. Pete got into it too and we settled into getting the job done.

The weather was perfect, pleasantly warm but the sun wasn't out draining all our energy. What a lovely way to spend a day. I certainly would never have thought of doing 'Go Ape' if it wasn't for these challenges!

When we got to some obstacles there was an option of 'medium' or 'difficult'. I was well up for this now, so you can see from the next photo that I chose 'difficult' – great fun, absolutely loved it! The hardest obstacle I found was traversing the vertical cargo net, quite hard-going on the arms. Pete really struggled with this one, in fact he got a few rope burns on the inside of his forearms from where he was hanging on for dear life!

The first complete round took us one hour and 10 minutes and sections three, four and five for the second time took us one hour 50 minutes, so a total time of three hours to complete the mile. I think the length of time to do sections three, four and five for the second time was so long because we took our time as we were enjoying it so much. It was on this lap that Pete took the photos which weren't easy for him, as he had the camera stuffed into the pocket of his shorts and it's *not* a pocket camera! There was one obstacle I failed on, which was where you had to put your feet into stirrups. That bit was okay, but I couldn't get my feet out to move onto the next stirrup so I had to pull myself over with the pulley instead. Pete did much better than me on that obstacle. The Tarzan swing was also very challenging but great fun. I loved this challenge and I must try and do 'Go Ape' again one day! Thank goodness I go to boot camp.

Cost: £32 each plus £8.50 car park

27th June

I thought I might ache today but I don't and neither the does Pete, although the marks on his forearm look more obvious today, the bruising coming out I suppose. Good news – I lost 1.2 pounds overnight. Okay, so now I know what I have to do – push myself physically very hard every day!

28th June

We are off to Southsea today for my roller coaster challenge. We were going to go to the Isle of Wight as well but everything ran a bit later than it was meant to. We called in at Marks and Spencer and IKEA on our way down to Southsea, and of course it's impossible not to get distracted in those shops – there's so much lovely stuff!

We parked the car for three hours at the esplanade seafront which cost us £3.90. It was 2.15pm so three hours should be plenty of time to do this challenge, have an enjoyable walk and a late lunch. The weather was lovely and warm, and I always find there is something relaxing about being by the sea. Perhaps it's the sound of the waves coming in and out rhythmically, rather like a baby being held to its mother's chest is comforted by her heartbeat. Listen to me all deep and meaningful!

Before we ate I wanted to get the roller coaster ride over for obvious reasons. Pete bought me a wristband for £11.99 which gave me unlimited rides on any of the attractions at Clarence Pier. He didn't buy one for himself as he said he'd done the rides many times before.

Clarence Pier is unusual as it runs along the beach and not out to sea like most piers, and is therefore wider than it's long. The pier was opened to the public on 1st June1 861 but was always vulnerable, as it is so close to Southampton and Portsmouth, and on 10th January 1941 during the Second World War, it was totally destroyed by German bombs. The rebuild started in 1953 when the first pile of the reconstruction of the lower structure was driven, but the actual rebuilding started six years later in 1959. It was reopened on 1st June 1961 – exactly one hundred years after it was first opened to the public.

I was telling this nice man John about my challenge, and how I needed to find out the length of the track. Unfortunately nobody there knew, so he kindly promised to text me the next day with the track length as he assured me he could find out tomorrow morning. Good, just what I needed. So for now it fell to Pete to work out how many circuits I needed to do. He started pacing the length and width although obviously he couldn't measure the track exactly, but with all the ups and downs and the track doubling back on itself he reckoned five would do it, so that's what I did. I hoped he would manage to get some action shots which wouldn't be easy for him as I was going so fast!

It was great fun and after the first lap not even scary anymore. When it was time for my fifth and last lap I cheekily asked John if Pete could have a go. He was quite happy and came up with a really good idea. He told Pete to go in the first car and me in second one, that way Pete could turn round and take my photo – brilliant! It worked a treat as you can see!

Five laps completed and hopefully the mile – should find out tomorrow from John.

Cost: Parking £3.90. Ticket for the ride £11.99

29th June

Harry is now 31 but when he was 30 Pete and I bought him a tandem skydive voucher as we did for Marcus when he was 30. After several cancellations due to bad weather, today is the day! Harry was remarkably calm and took it all in his stride – he loved it! He said it was the best thrill ever! While we were there I sneaked off and booked my skydive which is going to be two weeks today, Sunday 13th July! I had a choice of jumping at 10,000 feet or 15,000 feet. I went for the 15,000 feet (If you're going to do it – do it!!) That's it then, committed myself. Oh my goodness I'm going to be so scared. I think I'll try and put it out of my mind – fat chance! I paid £390 which included a photographer. There is no way this is not going to be captured on film as I won't be doing it again! I had hoped to hear from John today, but nothing!

30th June

I phoned Clarence Pier information, who promised me they would try and find out the length of the Skyways track and phone me back. I do hope so.

JULY

1st July

A few days ago, I booked an open top bus ride through the New Forest for my bus challenge. The easier challenges like this I am trying to do in a more novel way. I could have just taken the bus to Basingstoke and be done with it. This way is better though, as my dad shares the challenge with us and it gives him a bit of an outing as well. Pete and I met Dad at Lyndhurst at 10.15am ready for our two hour tour which was leaving at 10:30am.

New Forest tours run three different routes – red, blue and green. As Dad lives close to the New Forest I let him choose which route he thought would be best. He chose red, so we were all ready to go.

The weather was settled but cloudy and the sun was in and out a bit, so we were all getting a little cold sitting on the top deck. We wished we had brought our top layers with us, but it was me who suggested we wouldn't need them, so on my advice we all left them in the car! It was really breezy, but being very British we just got on with it and didn't complain too much!

The bus stopped at various points throughout the route and one of the stops was Burley, which is a chocolate box village in the western heart of the New Forest. It boasts tea rooms, gift shops, art galleries and even a cider farm, and of course you have to jostle with the ponies who always gather in the village. They are canny, and know that where there are people there is bound to be food! Feeding the ponies is forbidden, and it's actually wise advice as they are not always friendly and you may get a nip or kick if you get too close!

A few people got off and fortunately that included those people who were sitting right at the front on the top deck. Dad, Pete and I moved forward to benefit from the plastic screen around the first couple of seats, which kept some of the wind off at least!

Throughout the tour there was a commentary pointing out things or landmarks along the way. I learnt that there are approximately 9000 animals in the New Forest – ponies obviously, but cattle, donkeys, sheep and pigs as well! The people that own these animals are called commoners. When we went through Fordingbridge, Dad noticed an interesting shape of the river, and said he would take himself back there one day to take some photos so he can paint the scene. He has painted many scenes of the local area, particularly the New Forest, Christchurch Harbour and Hengistbury Head. It's a lovely part of the country to live and Dad has lived down there now for 47 years. He knows his way around well but admitted that on this bus tour he went down roads he'd never been down before.

The three of us all thoroughly enjoyed the tour, but when we got back to Lyndhurst I confidently asked the driver how long the tour was in miles, and he didn't know! Of course I know it was far more than a mile, so the challenge was completed, but just for interest's sake I wouldn't mind knowing. I may have to ask Pete to work it out on the computer for me, but I absolutely hate having to ask him for help as I always feel I should be able to do it myself. Unfortunately in our relationship we are inclined to compete, but as my computer hates me I may have to concede.

This photo was taken just after we got on at Lyndhurst with just a few other people joining us. We ended our trip by having a lovely pub lunch in one of the local hostelries!

Cost: £14 for me and £11 for Dad and Pete

2nd July

I have been unsuccessful in finding out the length of the Skyway roller coaster at Southsea. John did not text me and unfortunately Clarence Pier information did not phone me back either. Perhaps it's a closely guarded secret! While Pete and I were there he worked out that the distance was approximately 450 metres, so as I rode the roller coaster five times that means I did 450x5 = 2250m which is plenty. Even if the roller coaster is only 400 metres in length I'm still okay.

6th July

My weight today is 11 stone and 7.6 pounds and my fat is 39%. Thank goodness I have lost 1.8 pounds, I'm happy with that! About a pound a week which is ideal, with an added bonus of shifting 1% fat! I do hope I can keep this up. I know it's slow going, but as long as the trend is downwards I can stay positive, and at the moment the trend is definitely downwards!

I am hoping to knock off another three challenges today. It is also now only one week until my skydive challenge. I have managed quite well to keep it out of my mind over the past week, although as the date gets closer I know it will prove more difficult. Pete and I are off to the Isle of Wight today. We invited Felix and Harry to join us, but Felix has some Business Studies homework to do, and Harry has made arrangements to play golf. Felix is going to Nottingham Trent University in September to study Business Studies with Marketing. To help him on his way he is having a few private lessons to give him a head start – well that's the plan!

Pete drove us to Portsmouth Harbour. We parked at Gunwharf

Quays and walked down to the ferry terminal where we bought our tickets for the Whitelink Catamaran, which was due to leave at 11.15am. We had 30 minutes to wait but the man on the ticket desk was so chatty the time soon passed.

The cost for one adult and one senior was £20.70 which was actually cheaper than the car ferry, much to the chatty man's surprise. He was obviously a great fan of the island as he was telling us all about it and the best places to go. Pete and I knew where we were going to go though, we were heading straight to Robin Hill Park where they have a toboggan run. We left Portsmouth at 11.20am and arrived at Ryde Pier Head at 11.40am, a journey of just 20 minutes. Ryde Pier is the oldest in the UK, and in the summer of 2014 it celebrated its 200th anniversary! It is 681 metres in length and is served by the island line train. Wightlink also offer two other routes – Yarmouth to Lymington and Fishbourne to Portsmouth – another day perhaps.

As you can see there were plenty of spare seats. I'm sure it won't be this quiet once the schools have broken up. Portsmouth to Ryde is a distance of seven miles so challenge 43, catamaran, done!

Cost: £20.70 for both of us

To get to Ryde Esplanade we boarded the electric railway to save our legs, and were soon on the seafront. Pete found out that to get to Robin Hill Park, which according to chatty man is in the middle of nowhere, we could get on the open top Downs Breezer bus tour. Well, as luck would have it, there was one at the esplanade about to leave. Of course it was not really lucky as I'm sure they're timed to coincide with the ferries arriving.

My ticket as an adult but not quite a senior was £10 and Pete's was £5. I suppose that is *one* advantage of reaching 60 – the fares and entrances into things are a bit cheaper. Though I can imagine me not owning up to such a grand age and be silly enough to pay the full adult price – I'm a bit daft like that! I know I won't be a bit happy to admit to being 60 – I thought 50 was bad enough!

We settled into our seats on the top deck of the bus, right at the front, and just managed to restrain ourselves from being the bus driver like you do when you are children. We listened to the commentary and enjoyed the ride. After about an hour we arrived at Robin Hill Park and Pete paid the entrance fee of £23 (£12.50 for me and £10.50 for him). It's a lovely park, perfect for families with children. One day we must bring our grandchildren here – if we ever get any that is! I remember Mum and Dad many years ago brought Marcus and Harry here for a day out.

We reached the toboggan run and saw this sign so I knew that I only needed to do the run four times.

Each run costs £1.50 so I cheekily negotiated a better price as I told the man who was manning the ride all about my challenge. He agreed to four runs for £5. I started gingerly while I got the measure of it, and Pete followed in the one behind but quite a distance back for safety reasons. By the time I got to the bottom he had caught me up so I must've been going really slowly. Sometimes I surprise myself by being such a scaredy-cat! Let's hope I can summon more courage than this next Sunday! Second, third and fourth runs were much better as I gained confidence and there was no way Pete would have caught me, but he was on photography duties now!

Maximum speed of this toboggan run is 22mph as it's really meant for children, or adults who are young at heart like me! Easy peasy!

Cost: £23 (entrance x 2) +£5 for me. Pete got his ride for free.

The third challenge I set myself for our day out today was to do a mile on a slide. This was located right next door to the toboggan run. There were one or two children on it, but not too busy at all. Pete worked out that to complete the mile I would have to go down the slide 41 times! I started but soon realised that it would take me ages. I managed six slides before I gave up! The problem was climbing the steps to get to the top, which for some reason I was finding really hard. It was also not fair to Pete to expect him to just hang around and wait for me. Having abandoned the slide idea, we sought out a cafe for a late lunch as it was now gone 3pm, and we hadn't had anything to eat since breakfast!

We left Robin Hill Park and waited just a few minutes for the tour bus again, which I think picks up passengers from there every 30 minutes. As we had done most of the tour beforehand it was only a 20 minute journey before we arrived back at Ryde. This time we needed to return to Portsmouth by hovercraft which would now be my third challenge of the day. The Ryde to Southsea hovercraft is operated by Hovertravel, who are the world's oldest hovercraft operators. They are the only passenger hovercraft company currently operating in Europe, since Hoverspeed stopped using its craft in favour of catamarans. The crossing time of less than 10 minutes makes it the fastest route across the Solent from land to land. The timetable is only stopped if the wind reaches gale force 8 and above. Looking forward, Hovertravel has confirmed plans for two new craft of completely new design, with the first one to enter service in 2015 and the second in 2016.

As we approached the esplanade we noticed that the hovercraft was already in. Pete dashed off the bus to get tickets while I hung back a bit to take the photo, as I had a good view from up there.

I ran and caught him up, while he was just paying the £26.10 for our two single tickets back to Southsea.

There was just time for one last photo as I boarded the hovercraft back to Southsea. Journey time was 10 minutes – what a way to travel!

Cost £26.10 (both of us)

We fully intended to walk back to our car which was parked at Portsmouth Gunwharf Quays. In fact it is a lovely walk along the seafront, but after alighting from the hovercraft we noticed that there was a bus waiting. Being lazy we jumped on that, and only had to pay for me at a cost of £1.60 as poor Pete is already a senior citizen! An hour later we arrived home and settled down to watch the men's Wimbledon final which I'm pleased to say Felix had remembered to record for us!

10th July

One thing that I have always wanted to do is to visit the Ice Hotel in Sweden. Pete surprised me today by saying he would like to take me, and we could use dog sleighing and snowmobile as a couple of my 60 challenges. Of course, the visit would have to be in December as this challenge has to be completed in this calendar year of 2014. Well, I'm the sort of person who gets completely stressed out about Christmas, so I don't jump at the idea. However, after mulling it over for a day or so, I think after Christmas but before the end of 2014 could be a possibility! The thing that bothers me the most is that it is cutting it very fine and close to the end of the year to complete my challenges. I decide after much thought that I will go ahead with my '60', and when I do my book I will substitute one or two of the challenges with the one or possibly two from the Ice Hotel trip.

The important thing is to get the challenges done as soon as I can, as I'm not keen on leaving one or two of them until the last few days of the year. Just supposing we got there and all the dogs were ill? Unlikely I know, but I can't take the risk, I must get my challenges done first. With all this hesitating I do hope I don't come across as ungrateful, as that's the last thing I am. I've always wanted to go to the Ice Hotel and how lovely of Pete to suggest it. I tell Pete that I'd love to go and leave it up to him to arrange it.

The other good thing about this trip is that it I would miss Harry's birthday on the 27th and therefore not be forced to go out for our traditional family birthday curry!

The boot camp that Felix and I go to is running a six week body transformation class, where you have to attend three times a week for six weeks. You also have to complete a food diary and totally commit to taking it seriously. In return they tell me I will lose between 12 and 24 pounds of fat... apparently! It costs £187 but the person who achieves the best transformation gets their money back! Only 12 people per class and only those who want to look slimmer, feel fitter and have more energy are suggested applicants. Sounds good, so I've signed up as I haven't lost a significant amount of weight yet (well actually I've lost 7.4 pounds since starting boot camp) but the thought of boosting this is quite exciting, and although I know it will be hard work I'm totally 'up for it'! I mustn't forget or lose focus that my aim is to be in a size 12 dress for my party in November! The course starts next Tuesday the 15th – aargh!!!!!

11th July

Today, Pete and I are booked to go on the Orient Express train to Canterbury. The Orient Express made its maiden journey from Paris to Vienna on June 5th, 1883. Nowadays there are several trains all under the heading of the Orient Express, who rebranded to Belmond from March of this year. They are Belmond British Pullman, Belmond Northern Belle, Venice Simplon Orient Express, Eastern and Oriental Express, and Belmond Royal Scotsman.

We were travelling on the British Pullman. Pete had always wanted to go on the Orient Express but I can't afford to take him to Venice, so he will have to make do with Canterbury! We arrived at Victoria in good time so we could take some photos before we left at 10.45am. It was so interesting 'people watching'. Everyone was dressed up, several men are wearing straw boaters and bow ties and the women were all looking very stylish. Some were dressed from the 1930s period which was considered the 'golden period', but most were in summer dresses and as that is what I was wearing I didn't feel out of place, fortunately. We checked in and then a coffee was served on the platform by pristine white-clothed staff. We took a few photographs on the platform, and then this woman asked us if we would like a photo of Pete and I together. As we knew we had been allocated seats in 'Gwen' we decide to stand outside our carriage and pose.

Gwen used to be a carriage on the Brighton Belle which was taken out of service in 1972. Gwen was built in 1932 and had a sumptuous interior with plush carpets, velvet upholstery, marquetry panels, frosted glass lampshades and brass fittings. In 1948 she conveyed the late Queen Mother to Brighton. Maybe my seat is the very same! After being taken out of service, Gwen was preserved as a dining room at the Horseless Carriage Restaurant in Chingford Hatch, and later took up residence as an attraction at the Colne Valley Railway, Essex. Fortunately Gwen was acquired by the VSOE (Venice Simplon Orient Express) in 1988 and painstakingly and expertly restored. She joined the British Pullman 11 years later.

We boarded the train and settled into our armchairs – this is the way to travel! We got underway and the waitress (not the correct word as she was so much more than that) served us brunch. The table was beautifully laid with silver cutlery, fine bone china and startling white table linen. First, we were served a glass of Bellini followed by fresh fruit salad. After polishing that off, we then were treated to smoked salmon, scrambled egg, mushrooms and a crumpet – absolutely lovely! I always overcook scrambled eggs, but this was perfect. There was lots of English tea to drink while we soaked up the atmosphere, all the while whizzing through the outskirts of London and into the Garden of England – Kent.

Two hours later we pulled up in Canterbury where we were greeted by our guide Anthea, who took us by coach to the cathedral. We were left on our own to explore, with instructions to meet back at the coach in two hours. We wandered around the cathedral, but unfortunately we couldn't go into the nave as there was a funeral going on for some famous woman writer.

We took the opportunity while there to ask if we could climb the steps to the tower, but the answer was no as we would need to have someone with us, and anyhow it was only opened very occasionally to visitors.

We had time for a short stroll around Canterbury's cobbled streets before meeting our coach and making our way to Folkestone where we would re-join the train. The reason for this was that most people didn't get off at Canterbury but were going on to Venice, hence why the train was at Folkestone, as the passengers disembarked there to get their ferry to Calais.

On the journey home an English cream tea was served. It consisted of finger sandwiches, two mini scones, each with jam and cream and this tray of cakes – four each!

Pete didn't want his fourth cake so I ate it! I know I shouldn't have and I instantly regretted it; after five cakes I started to feel very crampy in the stomach area. Let's just say without going into details that I had to keep visiting the loo! I was so cross with myself for being so greedy!

We arrived back at London Victoria at 5.40pm. Rush hour at Victoria Station is not a good place to be! We managed to get on the first train going to Clapham Junction but there was only standing room, and while we patiently waited for the train to leave a voice came over the tannoy saying they were having trouble with the doors and were waiting for an engineer to arrive! Pete suggested leaving, but I voted we stayed put so that's what we did. Hard to leave now anyway as more people had crammed themselves in. Twenty minutes later the train left with, I'm pleased to say, the doors closed! At Clapham Junction we changed for a train to Woking, then from Woking caught a train home. What a day!

Just water for me as my stomach was still very unsettled. I hope I've learnt my lesson not to be so greedy, but I suspect I haven't!

Cost £377.99 (both of us)

13th July

The day I've been dreading has arrived! The weather is cloudy but I don't get a phone call so we leave at 1pm ready to be at the airfield by 2pm. Felix is coming with us and we are picking up Harry on the way. I'd like to think they are coming to support me but I suspect they think I'm going to bottle it and they want to be there to laugh at my humiliation, although maybe I'm being a little bit unfair to them.

On our way to Old Sarum which is near Salisbury I received an email saying that the sky-dive may be cancelled due to the thick cloud over the airfield. They suggested we could rebook but as we were more than half way there we continued with our journey, hoping we weren't wasting our time!

On arrival, we saw loads of people there as they had only had one flight and all the morning flights had now backed up. They were just about to continue with flight number two as the heavy clouds were shifting a bit, and they were confident that this would be the case for the whole of the afternoon. I checked in at reception and was told that I was booked in on flight number eight. They weren't sure I would be able to jump today as the airfield closes at 7pm and they had a lot of people to get through. Pete started to time the turnaround time, and as there was only one plane flying each turnaround took about 45 minutes so we knew it was going to be tight!

Marcus and Isabell turned up a few minutes after us and we all settled down for a long wait. If nothing else I would at least get the training done, even if there wasn't enough time for me to do the jump. I did however, keep my fingers tightly crossed I would get to do it today, as

I was so worked up I don't think I could have just gone home, only to come back the next week – my nerves would be in total shreds!

We all disappeared into the on-site cafe where the family tucked into tea, coffee, cakes, Mars bars etc. while I just sipped on water as my mouth was so dry!

After a while my name was called out over the tannoy along with someone else, requesting us to proceed to the briefing room for our training. That was straightforward enough and Paul the instructor was brilliant. He regaled us with the story of when he took his mum for a skydive, and after giving her comprehensive training about what to do on leaving the plane, she apparently screamed loudly with arms and legs flailing wildly about, all the way down! This story made as both laugh, and we both felt we could do better than that! Following on from the training was the long wait, but the sun was now shining so we sat outside and Isabell and I worked on our tans. I had to keep sipping water due to an unbelievably dry mouth as the nerves were really kicking in now.

Pete drifted off and asked at the reception desk about my chances of doing my parachute jump today, only to be told that I was booked on the next jump! Apparently several people had left and rebooked rather than wait, so I got moved up the queue. The next jump was number seven and my turn to show what I was made of! My name was called over the tannoy along with five others to go and get kitted up.

Oh my god, I thought was hyperventilating! I was trying to play it cool but it was not working. I was given some dungarees and then given help to climb into my harness. Outfits completed with hat and goggles and I was ready to go! When I say 'ready' I mean physically, as mentally I was a long way off ready! Paul knew I was nervous and he kindly came over to check on me. As I tried to answer him, my eyes welled up and I nearly broke as I told him how scared I was. He was lovely and reassured me that it really would be okay and I was in good hands. I knew that really it was just the freefall at 120mph that was frightening me – I knew I'd be okay once the parachute was open.

I don't know why, but Pete thought he would take my pulse at this juncture by feeling my wrist for 15 seconds then multiplying by four.

Well, my poor heart was beating at 120bpm and I wasn't even on the plane yet! We are all shepherded into a compound with a sign saying, 'skydivers only'. (That's me then!) Some of the people in my group were jumping from 10,000 feet and some 15,000 feet like me.

Everyone boarded the plane apart from me, I was left waiting for my tandem skydiver Lee who had just returned from his previous jump of 15,000 feet. There must have only been one person doing 15,000 feet on the previous jump as Lee came rushing back on his own, smiled broadly at me, grabbed a new parachute and came to greet me along with Rob the photographer. Paul must have mentioned I was very nervous as from the outset he was trying to make me laugh.

Rob talked to me while filming, hoping I'd say how much I was looking forward to it, but the truth is I was not! I just wanted to get it over and done with. The family wished me luck and the three of us boarded the plane. We had to sit well inside the plane as the people jumping from 10,000 feet had to obviously be nearer the door. Up and up we went, and after 15 minutes or so the door was opened as we had reached 10,000 feet and the height of our first discharge of nervous passengers. There was a strange quiet on the plane as the people who were excited and laughing just a few minutes before were suddenly very serious realising the enormity of what they were about to do!

One by one they shuffled forward and disappeared from view. There was no screaming or panic, just silence, so I guessed it wouldn't be appropriate for me to get hysterical. I had asked Paul earlier about the safety record at this airfield and it was 100% – no-one had died. It was a comforting thought, which sustained me in those final few minutes while we climbed another 5000 feet. After three minutes a red light came on which warned the professional skydivers that we were only two minutes away from the drop zone. Lee started to recheck all of my fastenings and harnesses and tightened everything really tightly, but I wasn't complaining – I mean who would? Lee was great and chatted to me all the way up. He is such a nice guy. He does this job four days a week and gets a buzz every time. He tells me he never tires of it and claims to have the best job in the world. Not sure I would agree but he loves it. He spends the other three days with his wife and children. In his words he's 'not rich but he's happy!' Good for him I say! The time was 5.50pm, the door opened and Lee edged us forward. We were the first of the remaining three to go. Rob was outside the plane pointing the camera at me so I tried to smile but it looks forced and not very natural but it was the best I could do in the circumstances!

We were now on the edge of the plane, but only for a split second before falling through the door into the sky below! Although in the photo I am upside down Lee did manage to right us, and we fell at 120mph for 2 miles which took one minute – unbelievable!

It's a strange feeling as I had no sense of tremendous speed, although of course you feel the wind buffeting your face. I didn't feel like I was dropping like a stone – funny really!

I was suddenly aware of Rob in front of me pulling faces and encouraging me to respond, but I was scared to let go of the straps that I was clinging onto for dear life. Lee put his hand on mine encouraging me to let go and I bravely managed to put my hands up as you can see.

I also managed to blow Rob a kiss and do a thumbs up! The chute was deployed for the last mile which was the only bit where I screamed. The shock element of the sudden change of pace was awful, and took me completely by surprise although it shouldn't really have been unexpected! We got yanked upwards but I soon settled into it, as we took four and a half minutes to drift gracefully back to earth under our life-saving canopy! This bit I guess I did enjoy, but the whole experience was so overwhelming, and I just felt so grateful to see the landing circle and to know it was nearly over. I lifted my legs for the landing and Lee took charge. We were down – thank the Lord! Lee told me to stand up and immediately Rob was in front of me with the camera.

He was probably hoping I was going to say, 'I loved it, I want to do it again,' but I think I only managed to say, 'I'm glad it's over'!

Rob and Lee were great throughout, and I particularly loved it when Lee kept saying 'good girl' to me – it made me feel young which is just what I need when I'm fast approaching 60!

We all got in the white rescue van back to the base where my family were eagerly waiting for me. Lee told everyone in the van about my challenge and they all agreed it was a brilliant idea! My family were more excited than I was, and so proud – I liked that! I wouldn't do it again, but *if* I did for some reason I would try and enjoy it more and not let my nerves take over, because it *is* a big deal, and I for one feel quite proud of myself for having achieved this. It was definitely my hardest challenge, and certainly the most challenging mentally! On the way home I texted my friends, who made me promise to let them know how I got on. Before I could text one particular friend she sent me a text: 'How's the hospital food?' Ha ha very funny!

Cost: £390

20th July

Hurray the trend is still downwards as my weight is 11 stone and 6.6 pounds. My body fat is 39.5%. The aim was to lose a pound per week and in the last two weeks I should have lost two pounds but only lost one. I'm disappointed but my weight is still down a little so I guess that's okay. I'll still make a size 12 by November! (Fighting talk!)

24th July

The last few days have been really hot, and we were meant to be taking Dad to the Black Country Museum today, but he phoned up last night and cancelled. He said that in this heat it would be too much for him, and looking at the temperatures today he was right! We have postponed it until September when hopefully it will be a bit cooler for him.

This coming Sunday we are having a big barbecue for about 20 of our friends and I have been busy preparing for that. I didn't include today in my planning as I knew we'd be out, so as today is a bit of a bonus Pete and I decide to do challenge number 48 – walking! As I found the skydive challenging I'm treating myself to a nice easy one today! We decided upon Virginia Water which is about 21 miles away.

This artificial lake was created in the 18th century under William Augustus Duke of Cumberland. The landscape design was developed during the reign of George III. Thomas Sandby (the renowned topographical draughtsman) was responsible for much of it. There are several things to look at while strolling around the lake, for example the Leptis Magna ruins installed by George IV, or alternatively the award winning Saville building completed in 2006. This stunning building was their first major addition to the landscape in the 21st-century. Virginia Water is located on the southern edge of Windsor Great Park near Ascot.

Pete and I walked around the lake knowing we were easily going to cover a mile, but as I wanted to know exactly, I used the sports tracker app on my mobile phone. We walked at a steady pace, stopping for photos and just taking the time to look, as life is always done in such a rush. It's good to slow down once in a while and notice all the lovely shrubs which are in flower, and how the light plays on the lake.

Our walk lasted for one hour and 54 minutes. There were so many little children on bicycles here, it was lovely to see. It was the perfect place for them with the smooth paths being completely flat. I told Pete that if or when we ever become grandparents we must bring the children here for a picnic and enjoy a lovely day out with them. When we had finished our walk my sports tracker registered 7.06km which equates to 4.3869 miles, but absolutely best of all, I had burned 621 calories!

Cost: £4 for the car park

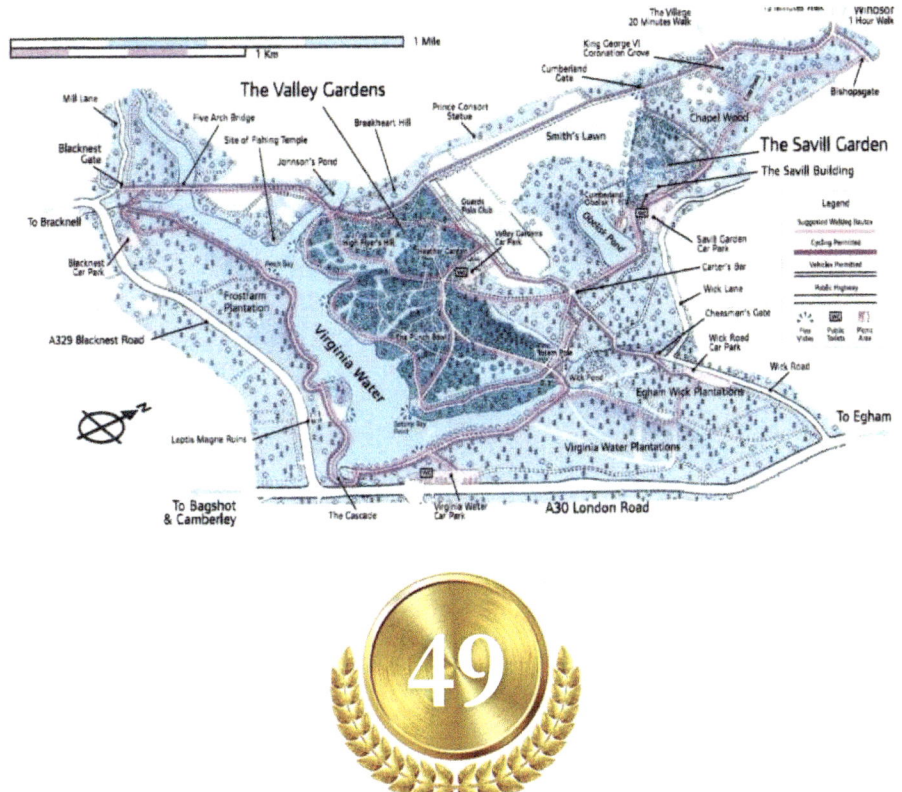

29th July

Today we are on our way to support my dad on the opening of his art exhibition in Highcliffe. It's not really his, but he is the chairman and has been for the last 20 years. Tonight is special, as he is going to step down at the end of the year so this is his last exhibition as chairman. On the way we are planning to do the driving challenge down the Ornamental Drive in the New Forest. It is situated between Brockenhurst and the busy A35.

There is not a lot I can say about the drive really, as I just drove down it and then back again. The photograph looks like there is no one driving the car, but I can assure you I *was* behind the wheel. Just to prove it, I stuck my arm out of the window to wave to Pete as I approached him which you may just be able to see.

The drive is lined with a mixture of large rhododendrons and azaleas and is best seen in late May or early June when it really is beautiful and attracts many visitors.

The ornamental Drive is also home to the largest trees in the New Forest.

There are two specimens of giant Sequoia trees – the largest one being 51 metres tall which makes it the tallest tree in the New Forest. They are native to North America where some have been measured at 94.8 metres tall and 17 metres in diameter. They can also live for 3500 years! So as tall as they are, they are clearly only babies, as they are only about 150 years old!

At the southern end of the Rhinefield Ornamental Drive is the entrance to Rhinefield House which was once a privately owned country mansion, but nowadays is a luxurious hotel. It was built in the second half of the 19th century, which is the same time that many non-native trees were planted along the track leading to the house. The year 1859 was when most of the trees lining the drive were planted. It is well worth a visit, as there are many walks on the Ornamental Drive – the most popular one being the 'Tall Trees Trail'. It is not a very imaginative title, but I guess it leaves the walker in no doubt about what they will find. Unfortunately, we didn't have time to do the walk today, but as Arnold Schwarzenegger said, 'I'll be back'! The length of the Ornamental Drive is 1.5 miles – easiest yet!

Cost: zero

AUGUST

3rd August

My weight today is a depressing 11 stone and 7.2 pounds. An increase of 0.6 of a pound! I know that's not much but it's the start of the slippery slope! I was meant to be knocking off a pound a week, so I should have been 11 stone and 4.6 pounds! I'm trying to think about what went wrong, and looking in my diary I see that since my last recorded weight on 20th July we have had a curry, a big barbecue for our friends, a Chinese takeaway and been to a wedding! Balanced against this, since 15th July I have been going to a 'Body Transformation Class' at boot camp which, take it from me, pushes me to my limits as it's so hard!

Even my fat has gone up 0.5% to 40%! A sad day – I'm not happy!

5th August

I have no work today, and the garden isn't *too* much of a mess so I have decided to do another one of my challenges. My friend Kate, who is one of my neighbours, promised me a while ago that I could borrow her son Jamie's scooter whenever I was ready. I phoned her up and she was happy for me to borrow it after lunch. Her son Jamie was poorly today, so he wouldn't be using it. The mile route I used before on the wheelchair and mobility scooter challenge has a hill along it, so Pete and I thought of another road near us which is flat. The road we've chosen is not so busy, and more importantly I'd be less likely to see someone I knew!

First of all, before collecting the scooter, Pete and I clocked the distance in the car. We did half a mile between a telegraph pole and some cross roads, so there and back would be our mile!

It must be all of 50 years since I was last on a scooter, so I had a little practice on Kate's drive first. Surprisingly it must be like riding a bike, as I didn't find it hard at all! A couple of other neighbours wandered over and started giving me suggestions for other methods of travelling a mile, for example 'space hopper'! I actually liked this idea, but as I have my list now I thought it best to stick with it, but it's certainly one to bear in mind if I need a spare!

Pete and I walked to our starting point carrying the scooter, and when we reached the telegraph pole I started. The road was easier to scoot along than the pavement, so I tentatively started and felt quite confident - that is until I saw a removal van up the road with three lads staring at me as I approached. I thought about making some sort of witty comment as I went past, but decided instead to ignore them and definitely not catch their eye! I got away with it, but I'm almost certain they made a comment about me as I passed. Probably said something like, 'Isn't she a bit too old to be riding a pedal scooter?' or 'Look at her trying to hang onto her youth!' Still, I don't care, and what you don't know doesn't hurt you!

Peddling a scooter is only just faster than walking pace, in fact Pete worked out that I was travelling at just under four miles per hour. The first half a mile took me nine minutes and the return half a mile seven minutes.

This photograph was taken by Pete just as I was finishing. I think I definitely look a bit puffed but not too bad. The main problem was my left knee which was aching due to the tension on it, as I had to keep it in the same position and very steady so I didn't lose my balance. There is not much else to say really, except I'm so glad my vast weight on this little scooter didn't break it, leaving me with the expense of having to replace it! The next day after work I popped into the shops and bought a bag of sweets for Jamie. Just a little thank you to him for letting me borrow his scooter. I was pleased to find that he was feeling a lot better today.

Cost: zero

7th August

Yesterday when I returned the scooter to Kate, another neighbour Sophie walked past and asked how I was getting on with my challenges. We chatted for a while and I told her about my remaining challenges, and that I was well on target. Not just to get them done by the end of the year, but I should finish them by my birthday in

November. She came up with a couple of suggestions, for example 'egg and spoon', but I rejected that one as really it is just walking, but her second suggestion of riding in a supermarket trolley I thought was great, and free of course! I went home and told Pete who agreed it was a good idea. He thought we would need to advertise what I was doing as I would be a 59-year-old woman in a supermarket trolley, in a public place, so the t-shirt idea was born!

I found a local printer who would print me a t-shirt while I waited. The cost was £19 but printed front and back it was just what I wanted! Next stop was Tesco's at the Meadows in Camberley. I do have a Tesco's much closer to where I live, but I wasn't not prepared to totally humiliate myself on my doorstep, so the Tesco's I went to is 12 miles away. That way if I felt embarrassed then so what? I wouldn't know those people, and they didn't know me, so I was okay about it.

We arrived and went to the customer service desk where Susan served us; she laughed at the idea. She probably thought I was quite mad but I didn't care as I was determined to do this now! She phoned her customer services manager Julie, who came out to meet us with a big grin on her face – she had probably been laughing at my idea as well! I like to think they were just jealous and wished they had thought of my challenge idea.

Anyway, after promising to stay on Tesco paths to ensure we were covered by their insurance, Julie was happy for us to go ahead. She was very keen to take a photograph of me, and said she would catch up with us later. I popped to the loo to put on my new t-shirt and Pete and I headed outside. Fortunately I had the foresight to bring a cushion with me to save my poor knees from the metal bars of the trolley.

I had to stand on a bench to enable me to get in, and as Pete was taking the photo this nice security man gave me a helping hand by holding the trolley steady for me. I was definitely feeling a little embarrassed at this stage, but so determined and pleased to be getting another challenge done. To work out the distance we used the sports tracker app on my phone. Pete started pushing me at 2.13pm right along the front of Tesco's and Marks and Spencer's which is next-door. I was kneeling up so my T-shirt slogan could be read, and of course we got loads of funny looks from people passing by.

If people smiled Pete just grinned at them and said, 'Don't ask, she's mad!' Well of course I'm not – spirited maybe but not mad! I think Pete must have got bored just going up and down outside the store, because he suddenly shot inside the store and started going up and down the aisles! Now this really was feeling awkward and embarrassing! From Pete's point of view though he found it much easier to push me due to the smooth floor.

Julie, camera in hand, suddenly appeared and wanted to take our photo. That's nice I thought. Well, I thought it was nice until she said she was going to put it on Twitter! Oh my god! Does that mean everyone could see me? I get very baffled by technology and don't really know what Twitter is, but what I do know is that if I start to get funny looks around where I live I won't be that happy! I'm supposed to be a respectable middle-aged woman ageing gracefully, not some sad woman afraid to let go of her youth!

When we had finished, my sports tracker registered that we had travelled 1.61km, with an average speed of 3km. The time taken was 31.48 minutes, but we did stop for photos quite a lot. It also registered that 123 calories had been used, though of course by Pete and not me! A good, novel challenge, I enjoyed it very much.

Cost: zero

When we left we went into Marks and Spencer's and I found a nice black dress which I fancied for my party, as I'm planning on the theme being black and red. I tried on the size 14 and it was a perfect fit, however, my aim is to get into a size 12 without the help of support underwear!

What else could I do but to buy both! The 14 is for when the party is over and I can relax with regard to my weight, although I'm talking negatively which is naughty of me. The size 12 is what I'm aiming for, but as you can see I have a long way to go! I'm just not taking it seriously – why not I wonder? Pete measured the distance between the top parts of the zip on the size 12 and the distance was three inches! I have also found out that you need to lose approximately 10 pounds to drop a dress size, and as the 14 only just fits me I need to lose a stone! I have three months left, so about a pound a week should do it – this is so much harder than the challenges!

Where I am: size 14!   Where I want to be: size 12

15th August

Marcus is 33 today. How can that be? He was a baby not long ago! We are all off for a curry tonight as that is our family tradition!

Freddie, along with his friend Greg, has decided to 'get back to nature' and go and live in the woods in Scotland by Lake Katrine, build a tree house and be self-sufficient! The plan is to live there for a month and live off the land by catching rabbits and fishing in the Loch.

16th August

Pete and I are under strict instructions from Felix to disappear for a large part of today while he has his friends round for a bit of a social as a goodbye before he sets off for university.

We decide to go to London to climb some more steps in some iconic buildings and hopefully do one or two other challenges as well. Felix's friends weren't due until the afternoon, so as there was no great rush we went blackberry picking in the morning and managed to pick loads. They are now in the freezer waiting for me to make some apple and blackberry pies – yummy! We left home about 2pm and drive up to London with our first planned stop being the Monument.

Fortunately, we managed to park quite close and for free – that was a real bonus in London! We strolled round to the Monument which is the tallest isolated column in the world.

It was built between 1671 and 1677 to commemorate the Great Fire of London, and to celebrate the rebuilding of the city. Sir Christopher Wren and his friend Dr Robert Hooke designed the colossal fluted Doric column which was built in Portland stone. It is in the antique tradition with a gilded urn on the top. The monument is 202 feet (61 metres) high, which is the exact distance between it and the site in Pudding Lane where the fire began. It started on 2nd September 1666 and was finally extinguished on Wednesday, 5th September after the greater part of the city was destroyed. The only buildings to survive were those built of stone, such as the Guildhall. Fortunately, there was little loss of life for such a catastrophic fire. The total cost of the Monument was £13,450, 11 shillings and 9d. Today, 311 steps take you to a viewing platform 160 feet (48.7 metres) above the ground. Pete and I climbed the spiral staircase twice to knock a few more metres off my running total. With only one staircase we had to keep stopping to let people pass, which is always fun as you dance round each other!

You can see from this photo that there are little window seats to rest if you need to, but we were okay and reached the top in about four minutes both times. From the top we got a clear view of The Shard across the river. It was hard to take photos though as there is mesh all the way round to deter people from committing suicide, as six people jumped to their deaths between 1788 and 1842. The total number of metres left for the step challenge now is 669-48.7=620.30-48.7=571.60 to go!

Cost: £4 and Pete £2.70

After leaving the Monument The Shard was our next stop, where we hoped to be allowed to travel a mile in their lift. However, I still needed to travel a mile in a taxi, so now was as good an opportunity as ever. In Eastcheap I flagged one down, peered through the window and explained that I needed to go to The Shard but the journey must be at least a mile! You know when someone looks at you, and without them saying a word you know what they're thinking? Well that's the look I got, but I wasn't going to be put off – I didn't care if he thought I was mad – I'd got a challenge to complete!

Anyway, he agreed and Pete and I climbed into the back. When we were close, our driver, whose name I found out was Ron, realised that we hadn't done the mile, yet were nearly at The Shard. Being a good sport he suddenly did a big 180° turn, drove down Southwark Street the other way, and then did the same again – good for him! We arrived outside The Shard having completed 1.1 miles! The journey took nine minutes due to the traffic and lights etc, but another challenge done – eight to go!

You can see that Ron thinks I'm mad can't you?

Cost: £8.20 – we paid Ron £10

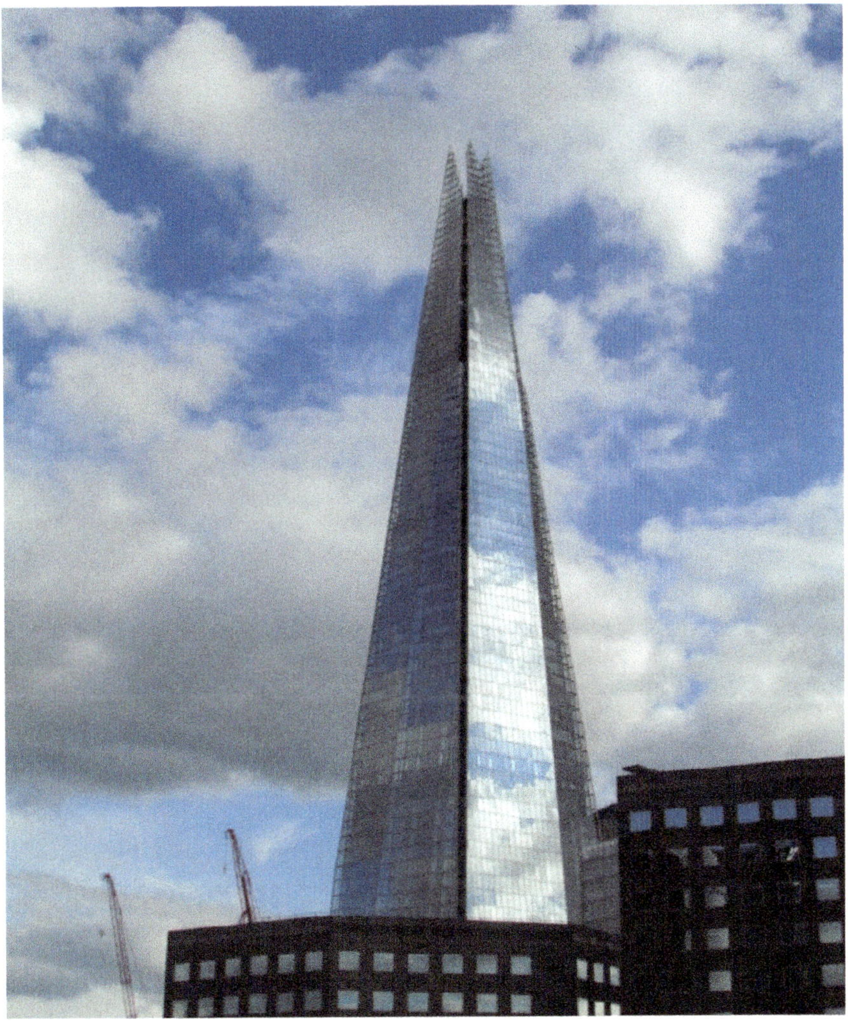

Before we go into The Shard, we pause to look and take a photograph of this magnificent structure.

It is a very impressive building. The exterior is covered by 11,000 glass panels which is the equivalent to eight football pitches. It is 95 storeys high, of which only 72 are habitable, and it is almost a third of a kilometre in height, being served by 44 lifts. It was designed by Italian architect Renzo Piano who said, 'I foresee the tower as a vertical city, for thousands of people to work in and enjoy.' It is currently the tallest building in the European Union, and was opened to the public on 1st February 2013. I knew to go right to the top we would have to book and pay £24.95 each, but we didn't want to do that so we were 'winging it'. We walked in a bit self-consciously, well I did anyway. Pete said, 'Look purposeful,' so I tried, but as I didn't know where I was going I knew I didn't look that purposeful so that plan didn't really work. I suspect we ended up looking rather shifty!

We made our way to the lift and went as far as we could, which happened to be the 35th floor. This level is the entrance to the Shangri-La Hotel. We ambled around as though we were guests and casually admired the view of course, and then luckily we spotted the concierge desk. A friendly looking young man was manning it, so I approached him hoping he would tell us how to best achieve my challenge. He was lovely, and quite amused by my challenge idea. He told us that we couldn't go all the way to the top, but we could do floors nought to 35 then take a different lift for floors 35 to 52. He found out for us that floor 52 is 220 metres from ground level, so Pete worked out that we would have to travel in both lifts eight times. I only want to count the 'ups' so, being prepared to be embarrassed, we started by going back down to the ground floor. Not much to say about this really as Pete and I just stood and waited for people to get in and out of the lift while we went up and down eight times.

The most embarrassing part was when we got down to ground level and the staff noticed that Pete and I weren't getting off along with everyone else. They kept asking us if we were okay, and as I didn't go into details about my challenge they must have just assumed we were 'lift freaks'! To ascend from ground level to floor 35 took 20 to 30 seconds, so with stoppages while people got on and off it took about 10 minutes in all.

The second lift took us from floor 35 to 52, where we had hoped to visit the Gong Bar to celebrate the completion with a drink, but when we had finished we couldn't get in because we hadn't booked! Oh well never mind, we could get a drink somewhere else. We journeyed from floor 35 up to floor 52 eight times, with the lift travelling at six metres per second. People were *so* nice as they kept saying 'after you' when we reached the top, but we had to say 'no, after you' so they wouldn't notice that we weren't in fact getting out! It felt a bit like a comic sketch. I half expected them to say 'no I insist, after you', but fortunately they didn't!

Total distance travelled 220x8 = 1760 metres – job done!

Cost: zero

17th August

At last I'm pleased to report that my weight has gone down a little. Today I am 11 stone and 4.6 pounds. That is a loss of 2.8 pounds in the last fortnight! Even my fat content has gone down by 1% to 39%. If I'm honest I'm quite surprised, as last night we all went out for a curry to celebrate Marcus's birthday. Maybe my body is peculiar in that I eat a curry and lose weight – now *that* really would be a clever trick!

23rd August

Today we are taking Felix to Nottingham Trent University which will be his home for the next three years! He is really excited and although I'm nervous for him, I allow his excitement to buoy me up! I have no doubts he can manage with the course, it's just his sight problem may prove challenging for him if he has to do a lot of reading. We couldn't be more proud of him, as he refuses to allow his problems to get in the way!

From Nottingham we drove up to Doncaster to stay with Dave who is a really good friend of ours. The afternoon was free for me, as I left Pete and Dave to have a good old catch up. I took myself off to Bawtry to have a stroll around the shops agreeing to meet the boys later. I found several clothes shops and enjoyed myself trying on loads of dresses for my party. I love the idea of buying a dress in an independent shop, just so no-one else has the same dress! Well, luck was on my side, as I fell in love with a little, black, flowery number. It had a sort of Latin feel about it, and was certainly different with button detailing around the neckline. I loved it! When Pete and Dave turned up I tried it on again to show them. They both thought it looked good so Pete bought it for me. The best bit of all was that it was 'one size', so no more worrying about getting into a size 12!

The next morning Pete had a radical idea! He said, 'Let's go on up to Scotland as we are halfway there and surprise Freddie and Greg!' Now I was not at all sure about this as we were not certain of their whereabouts but Pete said he was, so off we went! Without going into too much detail I'll just say that hours later, plus one speeding ticket, we arrived at Lake Katrine and spent four hours trying to find them! When we did, they weren't that keen on coming home (Greg was, Freddie wasn't!) but they *did* pack up their camp and come home with us as the lure of a hot meal and a decent bed was just too tempting! Apparently the only wildlife was hornets!

28th August

This is my last body transformation class and the results are in! Over the last six weeks of doing extreme boot camp three times a week I have lost the impressive amount of 1.8 pounds! Well what a waste of money that was, not to mention my time and effort! I believe it was my fault as you were also meant to eat healthily which is where I always slip up! Oh well I must at least be fitter now!

31st August

Oh dear, sadly my euphoria at finally losing a little weight has proved a little premature as today I weigh 11 stone and 5.8 pounds, and my fat has also gone back up to 40%.

Having already cancelled once, today is the day we are booked for a barge trip on the Basingstoke Canal. The barge we are going on is the 'John Pinkerton II'. We have our roast dinner at 12.30pm, which is 30 minutes earlier than usual. I am a little rigid in timings, and Sunday lunch is always a roast at 1pm – I'll try and cope!!!) Today, we have Freddie and Bronwen, a friend from university, joining us. I'm not quite sure whether Bronwen is just a friend or maybe more, but either way she is absolutely lovely and fits in so well. This was particularly well demonstrated last night, when Marcus and Isabell had a housewarming barbecue and Bronwen was chatting to everyone as though she'd known them for years! Youngsters nowadays are so confident!

Pete and I got to Colt Hill in Odiham for 2.30pm which is only about a 10 minute drive from us, so we could have had lunch at 1pm after all! Anyway, I'm over that now. It's good for me to try and be a bit more flexible even if it doesn't really sit that comfortably with me!

The barge trip was meant to last for about two and a half hours and I suspected this was going to seem like a really, really long time but it had to be done!

The purpose of the canal which was opened in 1794 was to increase trade between Hampshire and London. It is 37 miles long and was constructed in just six years by 200 men armed with shovels and wheelbarrows. This included building 29 locks, a 1230 yard tunnel, 69 bridges, five lock houses, four wharves and three warehouses! The canal struggled to survive on a commercial basis after the Southampton to London railway was built and it slowly fell into a state of dereliction. In the mid 1970s Hampshire and Surrey County Councils purchased it in a derelict condition following a campaign for public ownership by local residents. These same residents became a volunteer workforce, who restored the canal with the County Councils providing the funds and technical backup.

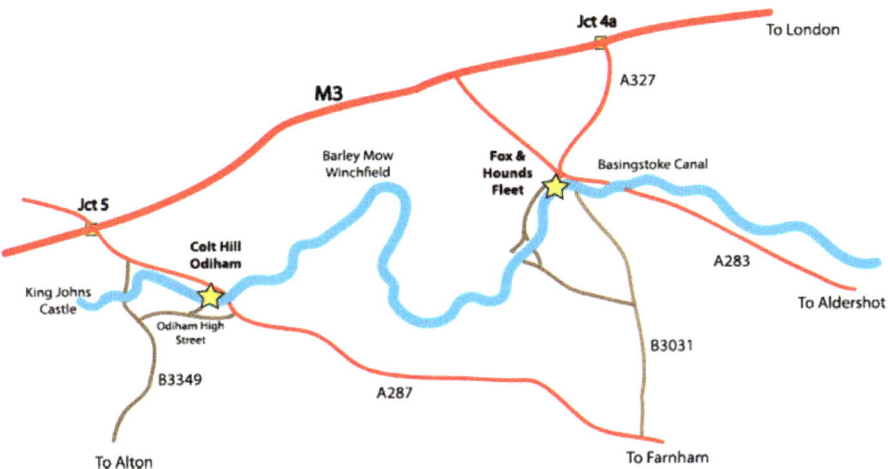

It was reopened in 1991 and runs from Basingstoke to just past Woking where it meets the River Wey. The trip Pete and I were doing was only up to the ruins of King John's Castle. Its name comes from the fact that King John stayed there for the night on his way to Runnymeade to sign the Magna Carta.

The distance according to Pete is 1.6 miles each way, and according to my sports tracker app we were travelling at 2.8kmh! That is slower than walking pace! I guess we had to go that slow to fill up two and a half hours! When we arrived at the castle ruins we were allowed to disembark for 20 minutes while the barge turned around ready to retrace our route. Although the barge was almost full, that is 50 passengers, not forgetting four crew members, I found it unbelievably boring, although I can see that the older and less able passengers would enjoy the slow pace of it all. I'm not 60 yet and certainly not ready for life this slow! The highlight for me was a nice cup of tea and a KitKat and a chat with Graham who was one of the crew, and husband to one of the Choral Society members that Pete belongs to. I wonder who John Pinkerton is?

Cost: £8 each

I phoned Laguna Park in Reading re the jet ski challenge. I spoke to John who was very helpful. I now needed to talk to Pete to see if he also wanted to have a go on a jet ski. It is £49 per half an hour. If it is just going to be me doing the mile I think I may be able to do it for free – that's the impression I got any way!

SEPTEMBER

7th September

For some reason Pete is not keen on doing the jet ski with me, so I ask Harry to come along. He says he may do it with me or not, depending on how he feels when he gets there! As it's the best offer I've got, it will have to do! John said we can do it at 2.30pm, but to get there for 2ish so we have time to get kitted out in wetsuits.

It's a lovely September day and we arrived at Laguna Park about 2.05pm. You can see the park from the M4 near junction 11, on the left as you head west. This we have done many times before when we've been to visit Freddie at Bristol's UWE University.

It was decision time for Harry, and I'm delighted to say that he decided to join me on the jet ski. I don't really understand why he hesitated; what could be nicer on a lovely day than bombing fast around the lake on a jet-ski? The cost for a half hour jet ski hire is normally £45, but as I was doing a personal challenge John said I could have it for £39 – how kind of him! Harry and I disappeared to our respective changing rooms to get kitted up in our wetsuits and lifejackets, just in case we took a nosedive into the lake, although it was definitely not on *my* agenda for the afternoon!

Laguna Park is a jet ski centre where you can either hire a jet ski or take your own, and today we were the only people who were hiring one. The one John gave us to use was a Yamaha Vx Deluxe with an 1100 cc stroke engine of approximately 110bhp. It was a 2005/2006 model. It had two modes, limp and unrestricted. Top speed in unrestricted mode is approximately 60mph, but we have to use it in limp mode so our top speed is 47mph.

John ran through all the safety issues with us and explained the course. Next, with me on the back, John rode the course so I could see where we had to go. It zig-zagged to the top of the lake, then straight across the top, then zig-zagged down the other side. John thought that twice round the course equalled 1.2 miles, but suggested I complete the course three times just to be sure. That was fine with me!

Now it was my turn with John on the back. How slow was I? I have never driven a jet ski before – I have always been tucked behind Pete when we've hired them on holidays in the past. I was going so slow it felt really unstable, and turning round the buoys was a series of jerking movements rather than the smooth movement it should be. John explained that more speed will make it more stable so I tried to speed up. We went back to the shoreline and John and Harry swapped places. I was much more confident now to do my challenge, in fact I was so confident I couldn't wait to get on with it! Three laps and I was

done! Harry was good company, encouraging me all the way, and on the straight at the top of the lake I reached the top speed of 21mph! The challenge took me eight minutes in total and I thoroughly enjoyed it!

We went back to the shore again for Harry and me to swap places, as it was now his turn to drive. As you can imagine, at 31 he was not so timid and we flew across the lake at top speed as if being chased by demons! I had to really concentrate just to hang on, as I didn't fancy a dip. I don't know how many laps we did, but it was at least 10 and great fun. Harry was trying to see how fast he could go and for a split second he hit 41mph! As I was feeling a lot more confident now I wanted another go, so again we went back to the shore and swapped drivers. I wasn't as fast as Harry for my last few laps, but I did for a brief second hit 38mph – yeah, happy with that! John waved to us from the bank, which was our signal that we had run out of time. We thanked him very much, particularly as I knew he had given us more than 30 minutes as it wasn't busy. Pete took quite a few photos including a couple of just the lake and no jet ski – I guess we were just too fast for him!

Cost: £39

9th September

My hot air balloon flight is due to take place at 5pm this afternoon. The arrangement is that I phone the weather line at 2pm to check if it can go ahead. The weather is still, warm and perfect, so I'm confident all will be well after the two previous flights were cancelled.

I was actually out for lunch with two close friends of mine, Kath and Anne, at a local hostelry, so I excused myself to make the call. I was pleased to hear that conditions were perfect, and the flight would be going ahead.

We were to be at the take-off site between 4.15 and 4.30pm. Winchfield Park was where we had to go to, so along with Pete and John, who is my next door neighbour, we drove to where we thought Winchfield Park was, only it wasn't! We asked directions from someone we saw sat in their car, but he had no idea either! In the end as time was ticking on, I phoned the booking line to be given directions. We had overshot the gate with the sign 'Adventure Balloons' on and now, because the gate was open, you couldn't see the sign anyway!

We arrived on site about 4.25pm. As with all these things there is a lot of hanging around and this didn't disappoint! The pilot – not sure if this is the correct term – was a man called Kim, who had his daughter Lily with him along for the ride. There were 16 of us in total, split into four sections in the basket. We all stood while Kim went through the safety briefing and what positions we had to adopt when he said 'prepare for landing'. Kim was a nice guy, but totally obsessed with control! I thought I was a control freak, but he could wipe the floor with me!

We all had to climb out of the basket and help with unpacking the balloon. All 16 of us had to spread it out on the field before it was attached to the basket. It took a long time and Pete and John took lots of photos and just hung around. However, I don't think they were too bored! Kim had made a line of cones in front of the entrance to the balloon which we were forbidden to cross, so when I called to John to come and take a photo inside the balloon, Kim told us off quite forcibly as we had crossed 'the line'. John and I reacted the only way we could, which was to retreat with our tail between our legs after sharing a glance up to heaven! We accept that we were wrong to cross the line, but it was only a tiny bit and the reaction was much stronger than we thought necessary!

At 5.30pm we were finally ready for take-off! We slowly lifted off the ground and ascended upwards over the treetops. Of course there is no steering in a hot air balloon, and we were at the mercy of the wind. Unfortunately this evening there was very little wind indeed. We drifted over the M3 and neatly ploughed fields with their pencil straight lines. It was beautifully calm and peaceful. The scene reminded me of a child's farm set, seeing all the miniature animals in the fields, then the coloured dinky cars on the roads. All my boys loved to play with when they were young.

For me, the most interesting part of the flight was when Kim had to contact RAF Odiham to let them know we were there, and also seeing Lily's excitement as we flew over her house, and she could wave to her brothers! Kim attached a camera to a frame outside the balloon, winched it into position, and then took this photo of us flying over England's 'Green and Pleasant land'!

The way the sun has caught me makes me look like a redhead. I'm not sure it suits me, so think I'll stick with dying my hair brown for now!

In these situations where you are thrown together with other people, you tend to chat to those next to you. The couple next to me came from Tadley, so I naturally said, 'My son Marcus is the manager of an estate agents there.' Well, their answer was unbelievable! Their daughter works in the same estate agents! I couldn't believe it, what are the chances of that? I was a bit worried then, just in case they didn't get on or something, so I tactfully steered the conversation in a different direction, but an amazing coincidence nonetheless!

After about 45 minutes of flying Kim started to look for somewhere to land, and was hoping to land in a school field in Odiham. The balloon had other ideas and drifted over the field to a nearby farm where Kim reckoned he could land safely in a wheat field he had spotted. The field had just been harvested, and now just the stubble remained. We were ordered to be silent and assume our landing positions, which in my case meant having my back to the way we were travelling. I briefly looked over my shoulder to watch us land, when I was told, 'Look forward like I told you!' Dictatorial or what!

I know he has the sole responsibility of the 16 people on board and I totally appreciate that, but he could have lightened up a bit!

We bumped hard onto the ground, but we were down safely so that's the main thing. Most people were allowed to climb out apart from four of us, me included, as Kim had to maintain some weight in the basket. (What was he implying?) The basket was then tipped onto its side so the balloon lay on the field ready for deflating. I must admit I hadn't given any thought about this process, but I certainly was not prepared for the 16 of us to have to squeeze the air out by rolling it up from the edges! All 16 of us worked on doing this, which was really hard and required a lot of physical effort. In all it took us about 45 minutes. Just before we started to roll up the balloon I was amused to see that on one side of it was printed 'Happy Birthday'.

How very appropriate for one of my 60th birthday challenges.

After the balloon had been packed away, we were each given a glass of Bucks Fizz or Champagne, and a certificate. There was now a lull in the proceedings so I took the opportunity to ask Kim how far we had travelled etc. He told me we had flown about four miles at anywhere between 0 and 5 knots and reached a maximum height of 2400 feet. Well at least another mile is completed, so that's good. A minibus came and picked all of us up and returned to Winchfield Park. Just as the minibus pulled into the field, Pete and John returned from having spent the last three hours in a pub, followed by a curry at a local curry house!

I think I'd rather have been with them, far too much faffing around for me! I won't be doing a balloon ride again in a hurry! I have since found out that what I had was a 'balloon experience' rather than just a balloon ride – well it was certainly that!

Cost: £120

14th September

It's like I've given up now that I have bought my 'one size' dress! My weight today is 11 stone 7.6 pounds, but on a slightly more positive note my fat has decreased by half a percent to 39.5%. I feel disappointed in myself because I should have done better. In the last two weeks I have eaten out six times! My problem is that when I eat out my willpower goes out of the window. Eating out is a treat and why spoil it by calorie counting? I don't believe there is anything wrong with that statement, as long as eating out is an occasional treat, but the problem for me is the frequency!

20th September

I had a lovely surprise today. Pete told me that for my actual 60th birthday in November he would like to take me to Paris! What's a girl to do? We talked about it and decided that climbing The Eiffel Tower steps could be the finale for the whole year and a great way to finish my challenges! I was planning on taking until the end of December to finish, but finishing on my actual 60th birthday seems just right and very appropriate – so that's settled then!

28th September

My weight today is 11 stone and 7 pounds exactly. My fat content is sitting at 40%. Enough said!!

Later today about 10am Pete and Harry are going up to Olympia in London to go to a Home Building, Renovation and Home Improvement Show. Freddie was meant to go with Pete as he is now doing a Master's Degree in Property Development and Planning. Unfortunately, he has booked to play a badminton competition, which is taking precedence as badminton is his first love! Hopefully though, Harry will find it interesting as working for Keyline as assistant manager it is important for him to keep up-to-date with all future developments and new products coming onto the market. As it has been two and a half weeks since my last challenge, I have decided to do my run/jog challenge before Pete and Harry leave for the day.

By 8.15am I was ready to go. Pete was also up, because as official photographer he had to come as well. Being a Sunday morning I'm sure he would rather have not felt quite so rushed. The route I'd planned to do is just around some local roads, which I've ran many times before, so I knew where the one mile mark was. The actual route is 1.5 miles. The plan was that I was going to use the sports tracker app on my phone to measure the distance and speed. Pete was going to follow in the car, and every now and then go ahead, park up, jump out of the car and get ready to take my photo as I ran towards him.

I set off, hoping I could do the mile without stopping. I wasn't sure I could, as although boot camp is great for making me fitter, I'm not sure it is very aerobic. We would see!

In this photo I had done about a quarter of a mile and I was feeling good. It really was so quiet. The only person I saw was one man walking his dog – where was everyone? Does everybody lie in on a Sunday morning? They really shouldn't, as this really is the best time of the day. I noticed that the trees were starting to show signs of changing colour, reminding us that autumn has just arrived. It won't be long before we put on our heating as the morning and evening temperatures drop. For now though the weather is very mild, luring us outdoors, before British summertime ends, the days become shorter and we draw our curtains at 4pm!

I reached the one mile mark and I was feeling good as I hadn't stopped. I kept plugging away and 19 minutes and 24 seconds later I reached my front door. My sports tracker told me I ran 1.5 miles!

It also registered my average speed at 7.2kmh which equates to 4.4739mph, which is hardly rushing, being just over walking pace, but I did keep it up for 1.5 miles! I look puffed and a bit red faced, but truth be known I could have kept going for longer, but no need to as the challenge was done!

I am nearing the end now as only three challenges left to go!

Cost: zero

OCTOBER

4th October

We have been enjoying a spell of fine, settled weather, so waking up today to rain was a bit of a shock. Unusually, we didn't have any commitments this weekend, so Pete and I thought we would take this opportunity to go to London, to see if we could complete more of my step challenge. Pete deliberated for a while as to whether we should go by train or car but the latter won. About a week ago, Pete and Harry went to Olympia and found parking no problem at all, so that's where Pete headed for, hoping that parking would be as easy this week. Unfortunately, when we got there we found the car park closed for some reason. Driving around we found a space at the side of the road which was free, as it was the weekend and a bit quieter – result!

Our plan was to head to Centre Point which is a 33 storey office block in the London Borough of Camden. It was one of the first skyscrapers to be built in London and, standing at 117 metres, it is the 27th tallest in the city. It was built between 1963 and 1966 but unfortunately remained empty until 1975. It occupies a site that was once a gallows, and directly below it is Tottenham Court Road tube station. The building was the headquarters of the CBI between July 1980 and March 2014. They have since moved to new offices in Cannon Street after more than 30 years at Centre Point. I think the scaffolding outside the building is something to do with the cross rail extension of the underground system, but I'm not sure.

We were there now, so fingers crossed we'd be allowed to climb Centre Point. We got the overground train from Olympia to Shepherd's Bush, and then eight stops on the Central line tube to Tottenham Court Road station. The tickets only cost us £4.80 each, which I thought was very reasonable.

When we entered we were greeted by a nice girl on reception, and we explained that we would very much like to climb the steps to the top of the building. She pointed us towards the lift, but when we emphasised that the lift wouldn't do, as we wanted to climb the steps, she said it wouldn't be possible! I cheekily ask her if she wouldn't mind asking her manager, and I magically pulled my challenge t-shirt out of my bag to prove I was serious and not joking. The manager eventually came down and agreed to let us, as long as a member of staff went with us. The poor waiter who was assigned to this task was Andreas who looked about 20 years old, very pleasant and smiley.

We started the climb at 12.24pm and Pete was given the job of counting the steps. Unbelievably, Andreas had his hands in his pockets throughout the whole climb, while I hung onto the banister for support and leverage!

We made it to the Paramount Restaurant which opened in 2008 and is the fifth highest restaurant in the UK. The restaurant is on level 32 and it only took us 10 minutes to climb there, arriving at 12.34pm. I was very pleased with that, particularly as I only stopped twice for a bit of a breather!

Andreas said that there was one more level up to the viewing gallery, so we struggled on up to the next level i.e. another 20 steps. When we returned to the restaurant Pete ordered us both a drink, while we sat by the window and soaked up the 360° views over the City of London. I was heartened when I glanced at Andreas and he was wiping his brow with his handkerchief – ah! Not quite so cool after all!

I asked Pete how many steps it was to the restaurant, and he reckoned 614, so with the extra 20 to the viewing gallery to add on, that totals 634 steps. We estimated the riser of the steps to be six inches so therefore 634x6 = 3,804 inches which equates to 105.66 yards or 96.616 metres. Left to do now is 571.60-96.61 equals 474.99 metres.

We thanked the staff very much and left. We made our way via the underground to Liverpool Street station and then to the Heron Tower. When we arrived, they didn't even have to think about their answer – it was no! The same answer was given at the Gherkin, and Tower 42, which is the new name for the NatWest Tower. I *can* understand their reluctance, as they don't know us at all. We may look harmless, and we are, but we *could* have an ulterior motive, and the safety of the building must obviously be paramount. Although I understand, it did leave us with no buildings to climb and still over 470 metres to do!

Feeling a little despondent a light lunch was needed, so we popped into Pret A Manger and had a toasted sandwich and coffee. I was tempted as usual and also had a muesli bar. Pete, who has a stronger will than me, managed to resist! It was there that it dawned on me that I had forgotten to take a photo of Centre Point – silly me! We retraced our steps back to Liverpool Street tube and then back to Tottenham Court Road station just to get the photo! How mad are we?

Struggling to think of where to go, in desperation we thought of going back to Covent Garden tube station and climbing the steps to ground level as many times as we could. We had done it before which is disappointing, but we were right out of ideas. So there we were, on this packed train when it whizzed straight through Covent Garden without stopping! Great! Now what?

A flash of inspiration struck me – let's get off at Knightsbridge and go to Harrods and climb the floors there!

The tube station is right outside Harrods which is all very convenient. Inside the store it was really busy, but I guess it always is. We found the stairs quickly and started to climb as far as we could which was up to the fifth floor. The first climb took us one minute and 28 seconds, not too bad at all. I counted the steps as we went, there are 96.

I felt a bit embarrassed when Pete took the photo, as people were looking at me and wondering who I was. We climbed this set of stairs four times which totalled 384 steps. When we had finished we looked around on the fifth floor and came across another set of staircases. These steps went down to the basement. Not wanting to miss an opportunity, we took the escalators down to the basement, found the same set of stairs and proceeded to climb up to the fifth floor again. This set took a bit longer to climb; two minutes 20 seconds and even longer by our fourth climb!

Again we counted them, and made the total 150 steps. My legs were definitely complaining now and I'd had enough, but I realised there was nothing in the photos that prove that I was in Harrods, so how about this?

I'm not sure what sort of large cat it is, maybe a puma, but I really think every home should have one! It is made from porcelain covered with platinum and encrusted with crystals and retails at £37,500!

The total height climbed at Harrods was 384x6 inches = 2304 inches +150x4 = 600x6 inches = 3600 inches. This totals to 5904 inches which works out to be 164 yards or 149.96 metres. The remaining total left to complete the step challenge is 474.99-149.96 = 325.03 metres.

We made our way back to the car and decided it was worth it, trekking up to London, but we both agreed that this challenge was proving to be much harder than we thought. With terrorism an ever present threat, I can totally understand why we weren't given free access to some of London's most prominent buildings.

Cost: £8.90 (tube tickets)

7th October

I phoned Martin Gosling, who is the man who promised to take me out in his tractor. I'm hopeful he will be in contact soon.

11th October

No news from Martin, and today we are off to Lisbon with four friends of ours for five days, so Martin will have to wait until we get back! Every year we go with our friends for a long weekend break and take it in turns to choose the destination. Our friend Jenny isn't a keen flyer so everywhere has to be within a two hour flight, well, that's what we tell her anyway! So if we suggest Malta for example, the flight is only two hours. If we suggest Dubrovnik the flight is only two hours, if we suggest New York the flight is only two hours, you get the idea? Jenny knows of course, but it's just a silly game we play!

We have been doing these trips for 18 years now, and they've been great. Some have been in the UK, for example Bath, London, Chester, and Blackpool, but mainly we have been chasing the sun in Seville, Prague, and Dubrovnik. When we first started these trips there used to be 10 of us, but recently the number has dropped to 6. This trip to

Lisbon will be our nineteenth, but more importantly the year 2015 will be our twentieth trip and we thought about going to New York! That would have been great, but unfortunately Pete (being a criminal!) will not be allowed to go, so we will have to think of somewhere else that is just as memorable! I personally think it would be good to return to the venue of our first trip, which was Paris, but we will have to go with the majority so that's a decision for the next year.

Back to this year – our friends Geoff and Vanessa picked us up at 6.45am for the journey to Gatwick. We arrived in good time and wandered around the terminal picking up magazines to read and sweets for the journey. The flight was uneventful (which is just what you want!) and *over* two hours, but we didn't tell Jenny, who I suspected was trying to sleep until it was over and we were safely back on firm land!

I was hopeful I would be able to do my horse and carriage challenge here, and also climb some more steps. The hotel was very well positioned in central Lisbon and our first impressions were good. The sun was shining which always helps, although over the next few days a lot of rain was forecast. We'd been so lucky with our previous trips and never had bad weather, but this trip I feared would be different!

12th October

Being in Lisbon I can't actually do my weight today! I could pretend it's 9 stone 7 pounds, but I fear those days of 9 stone something are well and truly behind me now!

Going by my clothes I suspect my weight is up a little, but not too much! I'm on holiday so who cares!

13th October

Today we went on the yellow bus tour to Belem. We knew that from here on fine days they have horse and carriage rides. Today is very showery, but at that moment the sun was shining so we searched around for them, but to no avail. We retreated into a café and asked the waiter if they would be going today. He lifted our spirits by confirming he had seen one just half an hour ago – great! We finished our coffee and headed up to where he assured us they started from, and sure enough we saw one waiting for a fare. There was only one horse and carriage, but that was all we needed, so we were happy! We climbed aboard and I asked the lady if she wouldn't mind taking our

photo. How lovely of the horse to pose for the photo also. I'm not sure if he's smiling or not, but at least he is looking straight at the camera.

His name is Flammie, he's 13 and from Belgium. We were taken on a 3km route around Belem, and as a mode of transport it's lovely, although not for those in a hurry! Twenty minutes later we were back at the start. It was very pleasant to view Belem to the sound of the horse's hooves clip clopping along the road, reminiscent of a bygone age!

The town of Belem is a shrine to Portugal's rich maritime history, and is crammed full of important historical buildings and national monuments. One of these is the Torre de Belem (Belem Tower) which was often the starting point for many seafarers as they set off on their voyages to the lands of Africa and the Orient. They were often gone for months at a time, and the tower became the symbol of protection and good luck for the sailors. It has served to meet the homesick sailors upon their return since the early 1500s. The tower was completed in 1520 and its structure has two distinct parts – the medieval tower and the modern bulwark. There are five floors with a terrace at the top, which provided the tower with a second level for the firing of artillery. Constructed on the edge of the Tagus River, it served as a fortress to guard the harbour, and since 1983 it has been listed as a World Heritage Site. The public are allowed to climb this tower, so I used the opportunity to add a few more metres to my step challenge. Pete and I went off to do this with our friends, and fortunately it was not crowded at all, which is always a plus on a spiral staircase! We were impressed to discover that they had a traffic light system in operation on the stairs which worked well. I wouldn't like to imagine what it would be like in the height of summer without it!

Due to the weather this photograph doesn't really do the tower justice, as it really is very white, which makes it stand out well against the Tagus River.

From the top terrace you can obviously see all around, as its main purpose was to protect the harbour from possible invaders. The tower has served two other functions – it has been a custom house and a lighthouse. There are 133 steps to the top of the tower, and the risers are about 7 inches, which equals 931 inches divided by 36 = 25.86 yards which works out at 23.64 metres. The total distance in steps left for us to climb is now 325.03-23.64 = 301.39 metres – getting there!

Cost: €5 each

Now that we were into climbing, we walked along the Tagus River to the Discovery Tower.

This monument commemorates Henry the Navigator, whose statue heads the line of figures which flank both of its sides. The figures include royalty, explorers, cartographers, scientists, artists and missionaries. The construction dates from 1960 which is when the 500th anniversary of the death of Henrique the Navigator was commemorated. He was the most important figure associated with 'The Great Age of Discovery'. Most people ascend to the top of this tower by lift but no such luxury for us! There are 267 steps to the top, and at 56 metres in height it shouldn't really be that much of a problem for us. I was shocked to find that I had to stop twice to catch my breath! Perhaps I was eating and drinking far too much on this Lisbon break. Could that be possible? When we finally got to the top it was disappointing to find that I couldn't see over because I am too short! What a midget I am at 5'2" My hand and lower arm were all that is visible to those below! Pete waved to our friends to prove we were there.

301.39-56=245.39. Great! Less than 300 metres to go!

Cost: €3 each

14th October

Another opportunity surfaces today to climb yet more steps. In the morning, we all get on the tram and go on a hill tour which we thoroughly enjoyed. We passed Saint George's Castle which is perched right on the top of the tallest of Lisbon's seven hills. The medieval castle is well known for its famous panoramic views of the city and surrounding countryside. It can be seen from almost anywhere in Lisbon.

The oldest parts date from the 6th century when it was fortified by the Romans, then the Visigoths, and eventually the Moors. It served as a Moorish royal residence until Portugal's first King Afonso Henriques captured it in 1147. He had the help of northern European crusaders on their way to the Holy Land. It was dedicated to Saint George, the patron saint of England. However, over the years most of the castle was destroyed, especially in the great earthquake of 1755, but there are still ramparts and 18 towers for visitors to climb.

The weather was miserable as we started our assent from the bottom of the town. Lots of flights of stairs, but because I didn't know the height of the castle I had to count them all. It took me 12 minutes to reach the top.

When we got there we paid to enter the castle, not really expecting very much, but it turned out to be really good. Fantastic views and, more importantly, there were loads of steps for me to climb. I rushed around climbing as many as I could, counting them as I went. After 600 steps I'd had enough and my calves were complaining. The riser of many of the steps was more than seven inches, but because I didn't want there to be any chance of me cheating, I used seven inches to work out how many metres I climbed.

In 1255 when Lisbon became the capital city, Saint George's Castle served as the Royal Palace, and the ruins were later rediscovered following major restoration work in 1938-40. The castle, having regained its former magnificence, was opened to the public, and it has been a National Monument since 1910.

The step challenge total now is 600x7 = 4200 inches divided by 36 equals 116.66 so in metres this equates to 106.67 metres. Left to do now is, 245.39-106.67 = 138.72 metres.

Cost: €5 each

26th October

Weight today is 11 stone and 7.2 pounds. My fat content is a gross 40%. It is almost identical to where it was 4 weeks ago! I fear that this is the weight I am going to be for my party! At least with a 'one size' dress I know it fits, so I will just have to resign myself to the situation I find myself in. I have zero willpower, and I just have to accept that my 60th birthday party was just not enough of an incentive!

28th October

Over the last few days I have been pestering Martin for my tractor ride. He eventually phoned me back, only to tell me that he had called round several times, but found me to be out. We agreed that today would be the day. I was barely out of the shower at 8.25am when Martin knocked on the door and said he was ready to go! I had sopping wet hair, but as Martin was doing us a big favour, albeit a little earlier than we would have liked, we agreed to meet him at 9am. He gave me directions to his nearby field and Pete and I arrived there at 8.55am. I had slipped a £20 note into my pocket, and as I got out of the car I felt for it, and was shocked to find that it was gone! Oh no! It must have been on the drive somewhere, or slipped down the side of the car seat – I'd look for it later. I told Pete, who fortunately had his wallet with him, and he kindly gave me another £20 note which I pushed hard into my pocket this time, as I didn't want a repeat!

Martin had his dog Barney with him, and as we neared the field we saw Eric (Martin's horse). There were 2x5 bar gates to climb over which posed no problem for us. I climbed the bars, then hooked my leg over the top and climbed down the bars on the other side. Pete on the other hand, did a sort of sideways leapfrog motion – very gazelle like! Martin's field is about a quarter of a mile round, so we decided to do five laps to be sure of the mile. His tractor is a Nuffield 465 which was manufactured in 1961. Martin told me that I was going to drive it, but I was not too sure about this, as I only drive an automatic car and I don't do gears! He assured me it would be fine, as he was going to put it in gear and I just had to steer it. That's okay then and we set off, slowly at first, but with only the steering to worry about I'm soon pushing to go faster.

To complete the five laps took me 11 minutes. It was great fun and another new experience for me. Barney kept running in front and Martin had to shout at him to get out of the way, as poor Barney didn't

realise that I didn't know how to stop! Dicing with death with me at the wheel is not a good idea! All too soon it was over and time to go home.

Martin posed with me in front of the tractor so Pete could get the photo, and as a bonus I was lucky enough to have a kiss planted on my cheek for my birthday! He wasn't at all keen to accept the £20 note, but after a bit of encouragement from us I'm pleased to say he did. I only have the rest of the steps challenge to finish now – nearly there!

On my actual birthday of November 12th Pete is taking me to Paris, where we will finish the step challenge by climbing the Eiffel Tower on my 60th birthday – couldn't be better!

Cost: £20 (plus £20 lost – I never did find it!)

NOVEMBER

8th November – PARTY DAY!

Over the last few weeks my best friend Kath has had a bad backache and been feeling very sick. Our mutual friend Anne and I have been very worried about her. Kath was last week admitted to hospital for tests, as the sickness isn't stopping. She is losing weight as she feels so sick and hasn't been eating. She came out of hospital today, and I had been pestering her husband Vic while she was in hospital for news, but was told by him that Kath wanted to tell me herself. I was hoping to see her before we went to the hotel where I was having my birthday party, but unfortunately I didn't get the chance.

My party started at 7.30pm and I have to admit to being quite relieved that I didn't see Kath beforehand. If it was bad news I just knew I wouldn't be able to put the news on one side and enjoy myself. I was very worried about her, but I had 56 guests coming to my party so I had to focus on getting organised!

Even though I was holding my party in a local hotel a lot of planning was involved. For the place settings I decided to have photographs of each of my guests on yellow easels – not as easy as you'd think, particularly when my nephew said he wanted to bring his girlfriend, and I didn't have a photo! Good old Facebook! I had to take some guests' photos from their Facebook profile, and one poor guest I just couldn't find a photo of at all. As he worked for Domino's Pizza, his place setting photo was a pizza with a smiley face on! I then had all the photos laminated ready for going on the easels, which had to be painted by hand as they arrived as bare wood. I was very happy with how they looked on the night fitting in with my yellow, green and white theme. I was going to have a black and red themed party but as the room was yellow and blue I had to have a rethink! As organised as I was, the day of my party was one of the most stressful ever!

I had a nail appointment in the next village about 3 miles away at 9am. I was meant to take the nail polish with me, but I forgot, so had to turn around and drive home and get it – not a good start. When I pulled up outside the salon for the second time, I found I couldn't switch the lights off on the car. I really tried but they just wouldn't turn off! I phoned Pete who drove up in the other car (my knight in shining armour!) to find out what the problem was. I was worried about having a flat battery when I came out of the salon. The answer was simple, and I should have known that when I indicated to pull into the layby I didn't actually turn the corner so the indicator was still on, and because of that the lights wouldn't turn off. Fortunately that's all it was – I felt a bit of a fool! The next minor irritation was when I went to my hairdresser Sarah. I had forgotten the hair slides I was meant to take with me, so yet again I had to drive home to retrieve them!

My brother David lives in Guernsey with his wife Gill and three sons. I was thrilled they were able to come over for my party and help me celebrate. Unfortunately though Alex, his youngest, can't come. Let's look at the reason – he has an invitation to his Aunt's 60th birthday party, but the opportunity had also arisen for a weekend in Marrakesh with the girlfriend. What to do? No contest!

David used to work for an airline based in Guernsey, so they were all booked on standby tickets. David and Gill flew into Gatwick with no problems, and they then had hired a car. The others were flying into Southampton Airport, but there were only two seats available so Robert and his girlfriend Astrid took those, leaving Daniel and his girlfriend Jo to get a flight to Birmingham, as there were no other flights to Southampton that day! That was inconvenient enough, but the plane got hit by a bird strike, which knocked out one of the propellers! Daniel from his window also saw bits fly off from the nosecone! The poor lad thought the plane was going down. He has told me since that it was the most frightening flight he had ever been on! After landing safely however, Daniel and Jo caught a train to Reading station, only to hear the announcement that all trains to Basingstoke had been cancelled due to flooding on the line. Poor Pete was dispatched to pick them up (knight in shining armour yet again!)

Meanwhile, Harry had to go and collect the balloons which was the job Pete was meant to be doing at that time, according to my time plan. It doesn't finish there, because when I was in the hotel room getting ready my phone rang. It was my Dad, who *should* have been on the train, saying that the taxi which was meant to pick him up never arrived! He had phoned a different company and was now just waiting for them; he was still coming but would be on a much later train – unbelievable! Pete got back from Reading station in time to shoot straight off to collect my Dad from Basingstoke – what a star Pete was that day!

Just to add to the mix the trains only went as far as Winchester as they were doing engineering works on the line, so Dad had to get the bus from Winchester to Basingstoke just to further complicate things. After all that, fortunately things calmed down. I was lucky enough to have a great party! Good food, DJ, a party game which consisted of each table having to name the 60 challenges I've done this year, and a table magician for entertainment. 'Happy Birthday' was sung to me while I cut a lovely birthday cake made for me by Sarah my hairdresser, which was totally amazing, what a talented woman she is!

I am on top of the cake having just done a boot camp session and all around the cake she has put some of the challenges I have done, e.g. mobility scooter, bike and at the back was a canoe! The bottom left is my fish pond which I love. She had even done a reference to my favourite shop!

To my surprise, I even managed a short speech which was as big a shock to me as my guests, because one of my big fears in life is public speaking! You can see from Pete's face that he's surprised I've done it, can't you? A great party – I loved it! Now Paris to look forward to…

I did fail in my challenge to fit into the size 12 dress which is disappointing, but hardly surprising considering the number of times I ate out and of course my love of food! Maybe next year with Marcus and Isabell's wedding on the horizon I can try again. The date they've set is July 18th – okay, that's seven months from January, that should be long enough to shift a stone. I can do this, can't I?

9th November

I couldn't actually weigh myself today because we spent the night in the hotel, but I weighed myself on the 10th and the scales read 11 stone 7.2 pounds, fat 40%!! This is the exact weight I was two weeks ago! Back in January I vowed to shift weight for my party – well technically I did as my weight has decreased by 7.6 pounds and my fat has reduced from 42% to 40%. I found out from somewhere, (I don't remember where now) that to go from a size 14 to a size 12 equates to a loss of 10 pounds in weight. If that is true, then I was only 2.4 pounds away from my target! I know I wanted to be in a size 12 dress and that I didn't manage it, but is it really my fault that the dress I fell in love with was 'one size'?

I phoned Kath today to ask if I could pop round. Even though I felt anxious that it may be bad news, I was not prepared for what she told me. She has pancreatic cancer and 6-12 months to live! I felt like I'd been slapped around the face, I felt so shocked! I gave her a hug as we both fought back the tears and I told her that I was so sorry this has happened to her. I wanted to tell her that it will be alright, but we both know it won't. I'm fumbling for words when she says, 'Let's just carry on as normal for as long as we can.' She asks me to be strong for her and I vow to do just that, it's the very least I can do for her. I want to cancel our trip to Paris but she absolutely insists we go – so go we will.

11th November

We are staying for two nights at the Napoleon Hotel near the Champs Elysees. Kath's news has cast a shadow over our couple of days away, but she would be cross if she knew, so we are going to endeavour to enjoy ourselves for her sake. Pete has really been spoiling me recently, and I love the idea of finishing my challenges by climbing the steps of the Eiffel Tower as my final ascent, and on my actual birthday as well! Bring it on…

12th November – MY SIXTIETH BIRTHDAY!!!!

My 60th birthday and my 60th challenge! All that I have left to finish them is to climb the final 138.72 metres of my step challenge. We decide to climb the South Tower of Notre Dame Cathedral first. Its height is 69 metres and it is reached by a stone spiral staircase. There is quite a queue to go in as they only let in 20 people at a time. We have to wait about 30 minutes, and I'm seriously regretting not taking a coat as I'm freezing, but just have to get on with it. The cathedral was built over a period of 200 years and its construction was initiated by Bishop Maurice de Sully around 1160. The South Tower houses the cathedral's largest bell, weighing more than 13 tons and even its clapper weighs 500kg. This 17th-century great bell is tuned to f sharp and is known as Emmanuel. It is only rung on major Catholic feast days, whereas the other four bells in the North Tower peal out several times a day. Pete and I struggled more than we expected to when climbing this, as there were 422 steps and little chance to pause and catch your breath, as there were constantly people behind you. You didn't want to be the one holding them up!

The photo was taken near the beginning of the climb, as I certainly wasn't looking this cool and smiley at the end! On reaching the top, Pete and I could hardly talk as we were panting so much but the view was magnificent! Every year about 13 million people from all over the world visit the cathedral, and on peak days that can be 50,000 visitors per day. Maybe some of them want to see the setting for Victor Hugo's famous novel 'The Hunchback of Notre Dame' which was first published in 1831. A large part of the novel's action takes place in the towers, with pride of place being given to the bells and their famous bell ringer Quasimodo. Since 1991 the cathedral has received the UNESCO World Heritage listing.

I only have 69.72 metres left to complete the step challenge.

Cost: €8.5 each.

Pete and I left Notre Dame and made our way by bateau to the Eiffel Tower. What a magnificent structure this symbol of Paris is, standing at 324 metres high, which is about the same as an 81 storey building. It was named after Gustave Eiffel whose company designed and built the tower, which is the tallest structure in Paris, and the most visited paid monument in the world. The tower received its 250 millionth visitor in 2010. It was erected in 1889 as the entrance arch to the 1889 World Fair. It was initially criticised by some of France's leading artists and intellectuals for its design, but it has become a global cultural icon of France, and one of the most recognisable structures in the world. It held the title of the tallest man-made structure in the world for 41 years until the Chrysler Building in New York City was built in 1930. Nowadays it is taller than the Chrysler Building by 5.2 metres because an aerial was added in 1957.

Our intention was to climb to the second floor which is a total climb of 115 metres. We set off at 15.49pm, and found this so much easier to climb than Notre Dame. For a start there are proper staircases and banisters, and a little landing after each flight of stairs if we needed to rest. Eight minutes and 328 steps later we were on the first floor. Not feeling bad-considering!

We looked around for a while taking in the view, then with excited anticipation of finishing the whole year-long challenge, we continued up to the second level. Obviously this is much the same as the first but 341 steps this time and seven minutes from level one to two.

We finished the whole challenge at 16.32pm on Wednesday 12th of November! I am really pleased as I thought it would take me the whole year to complete. I anticipated having a mad scramble in the last few days of 2014! Pete and I high five and as if by magic he produces a bottle of champagne out of his backpack to celebrate. I admit to being seriously tempted, but as we would have to drink the whole bottle and we had 669 steps back to ground level, I declined and said we'd have it later! Sometimes I think I miss out by being just too sensible! What a lovely gesture though!

That evening was spent on the Bateau Mouche cruising up the Seine while enjoying a superb meal and listening to a brilliant duo comprising a pianist and violinist. They played for about two hours while we took in the sights of Paris by night. What a birthday! What a husband, so supportive – he's great! (But his photography skills could be better!)

We got a stranger to take this photograph of us on level two with Paris in the background – perfect!

Cost: €5 each

And to finish…

This book is not a literary masterpiece and nor is it trying to be, but it is an accurate account of how my life has panned out over the past year. I haven't made things up or exaggerated anything, which is why some of it may seem a bit mundane and not very interesting! I did, however, on 12th November 2014, my 60th birthday, complete my challenges and this book has been the story of my journey.

I looked up the word 'challenge' in the dictionary, and as a noun it means 'A task or situation that tests someone's abilities.' My challenge, set by my friend Angie, was to complete 60 miles in a year by different methods, so I guess by me referring to each method as a challenge is strictly inaccurate, and I should really have used the word 'tasks' instead. Sixty tasks to complete one challenge. Oh well, it's too late now, but if I was doing it again that is something I would change. I mean, many of my tasks were easy, for example monorail, riverboat, drive: nobody could call these challenging at all.

For me the hardest task was waterskiing which I found very challenging physically, particularly on the arms and I never did make it to the back of the boat like a proper waterskier! I thought that this task was the one that I was going to fail on, but sheer grit and determination saw me through! The skydive was also challenging, not physically but mentally. I struggled with the terrifying thought of nearly three miles high, freefalling at over 100mph for two miles, and the fact that I was nearly 60! I seriously considered that the shock may just too much for me, and I might have a heart attack and die! See what I mean? Mentally that's quite a lot to get grips with!

My favourite challenge had to be the zip wire which was amazing, not a challenge at all, just good fun and really enjoyable. Pete and I are hoping to take my Dad there next year as he wants to do it now, but by next year he will be 89, although I believe the oldest person to do the zip wire was 94! This must be where I get my mad streak from!

The challenge I hated the most was the dry ski slope, it was awful! I kept falling over and felt totally unstable and out of control. I have never been skiing but always thought that one day I would, but if it is anything like that then I will happily give it a miss! This was a surprise to me, as I would not have expected this challenge to be the one I disliked the most, but I don't even need to consider any of the others for the title, as without a doubt the dry ski slope is not something I will ever be trying again!

The challenges I completed I chose myself and expected it to be quite hard thinking of 60 ways to travel a mile, but in fact most of them tripped off the tongue quite quickly. By the time Pete and I had eliminated some impossible ones, like abseiling, I was happy with the final list. For anyone reading this and feeling they would like to do something similar for their 70th birthday, then here are a few more suggestions which I didn't use: paragliding, slide, golf buggy, stretcher, rollerblades, space hopper, crutches, sledge, London Eye and so on... Why stop at 70?

Everybody I have met during this past year has been so supportive and encouraging and I can honestly say I have not received one negative comment! Well, maybe one from my Dad, who said I must be barmy and completely mad when I told him about my challenge back in January, but even he has capitulated and said he thinks it was a brilliant idea and I've done really well! He has taken on board the idea that I like to do different experiences, so for my 60th birthday he bought me a flying lesson which is slightly different to the Marks and Spencer voucher I was expecting!

One thing I would say is that doing these challenges was not cheap! All the way through I recorded how much we spent and obviously as Pete was with me, we had his costs as well. Below is the total of the costs for the 60 challenges. I consider it to be well worth it, as it was great entertainment for 11 months and such fun! These costs include odds like car parks, hotels and photographs when necessary. Also included are the costs for other people who shared my experience, for example Pete and my dad. Pete and I paid approximately half of these costs each.

£2087.97 plus €59

I wouldn't be surprised if some of the people I've spoken to do something similar themselves when they reach a landmark birthday, as they all loved the idea. One person said to me, 'Are you doing a blog?' Now I don't really know what a blog is, but my understanding is (having looked it up) that a blog is a publicly accessible personal journal which members of the public can comment on. The month I was asked if I was doing one was June so really too late to start a blog, but I wish I'd thought of it, as it would have been fun and good to get feedback. It's certainly something I would do if I was attempting anything like this again. I regret that I didn't think of it last January. My other big regret is that I was offered the chance to go on Radio Solent, but I declined due to my lack of confidence. That was a big mistake, as it would have been a good opportunity for me to promote what I was doing, fire people's interest, and hopefully, make people realise that you're never too old to do silly things and have fun!

Pete has done 29 of these challenges as well, and was with me on every one as photographer. I think he would say the step challenge was harder than we thought it would be, particularly as we struggled to find suitable high buildings to climb. The ones we did climb involved a lot of travelling, as there are not too many high buildings near where we live – well not notable buildings anyway! As for the rest of my family, they were supportive but I regret not involving them a lot more. Harry did do jet skiing with me, Felix walked backwards and skipped with me for some of the way, and Marcus, Isabell and Harry rode bikes with us through the New Forest. They are all busy people with their own lives to lead, and as Pete and I did most of the challenges during the week on the two days I don't work, it was difficult to involve them.

Next year, Pete and I are hoping to do the London to Brighton bike ride now that we have the challenge bug. As Marcus, Isabell and Harry live within five miles of us I think I might suggest we all do it together, as positive family times are valuable and create memories. I wonder how well that will go down with them when I suggest it?

My own feelings on having completed this challenge are that I thoroughly enjoyed every minute of it (well, nearly). As soon as Angie suggested it way back in January, I knew it was something I could do, as I loved the idea right from the start. I have a tendency to give up when things get hard, but I was so determined on this challenge there was no way I wouldn't complete it. The purpose was to do something positive after a difficult few years, and it was certainly that for Pete and me. It gave a real focus to our lives for the whole year, although that didn't extend to the rest of the family as I had hoped. A little bit silly of me to expect it to, I mean why would me doing challenges be a focus for them?

Most of the time we sort of drift through the years of our life, although I do always make a New Year's resolution list which I try my hardest to complete. I put on things like decorate spare room, redesign the garden, clear out kitchen cupboards etc, and every year there is *always* lose weight on the list. I usually complete most of the resolutions, but you won't need to be a rocket scientist to know which one I *always* fail. However, I enjoy having the focus as it helps me to achieve little accomplishments, which in turn help to make me feel good about myself. I believe we all like achieving things, not necessarily big, earth-shattering things, but the small successes of everyday living, which can still give a great feeling of satisfaction. Maybe it's not for everyone but it works for me!

Pete and I are lucky enough to be going to Sweden and the Ice Hotel at the end of the year. I had planned to swap two of the lesser challenges for snowmobile and dog sleigh but I'm not going to do that now, as I like the idea of finishing on my birthday, so I will leave things just as they are. Looking forward to next year, we have Marcus and Isabell's wedding in July. I'm hoping to lose weight for that, just like my mum did for mine, so here we go again! I'm hoping Harry will find a lovely girl, be really happy, and also become the manager of his own branch. Felix will be in his second year at university and working hard, I hope, and as for Freddie, he should have completed his Masters and entered the world of employment – fingers crossed! My dear friend Kath will have our love and prayers every day as she continues with her battle.

Doing this challenge has taught me not to be afraid of trying new things, as I'm stronger than I thought. My age of 60 is NOT going to be a barrier to embracing life – I'm not saying live every day like it's your last, but I am advocating making the most of every day because life is short. I'm lucky to enjoy good health and fortunate to have loads of energy, which I'm all too aware can easily be snatched away. You owe it to yourself to make the most of your life, so that you will have lots of happy memories to sustain you in your twilight years and not regrets for opportunities missed – go girl!

WHAT A YEAR! GREAT FUN!

Lightning Source UK Ltd.
Milton Keynes UK
UKOW07f1600100117
291777UK00012B/92/P